A HERO IS BORN.

Welles would reach for the bandanna on his desk or in his pocket, lift it above his head, and wave it in the air.

"He would say, 'This is where the magic comes from,'" Natalie recalled.

Other times—"I'm a superhero."

And once, facing some tall task, he lifted the bandanna, stood up from his chair, and made a preposterous declaration that Natalie never forgot.

"I'm going to save the world."

OTHER BOOKS YOU MAY ENJOY

The RED Bandanna

TOM RINALDI

PUFFIN BOOKS

PUFFIN BOOKS
An imprint of Penguin Random House LLC
375 Hudson Street
New York, New York 10014

First published in the United States of America by Viking,
an imprint of Penguin Random House LLC, 2017
This work is based on *The Red Bandanna* by Tom Rinaldi, copyright © 2016 by Tom Rinaldi,
published by Penguin Press, an imprint of Penguin Random House LLC.
Published by Puffin Books, an imprint of Penguin Random House LLC, 2018

PHOTO CREDITS:
Page 3: Jewel Samad / AFP / Getty Images
Pages 55, 75: Courtesy of Chuck Platz
Page 106: U.S. Navy / Getty Images News
Other photographs courtesy of the Crowther family

LIBRARY OF CONGRESS CATALOGING-IN-PUBLICATION DATA IS AVAILABLE
Puffin Books ISBN 9780425287644

Book design by Jim Hoover

Printed in the United States of America

9   10

for Dianne, the certainty.

for all, for whom the day endures.

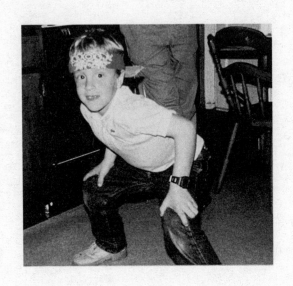

"You can hold back from the suffering of the world. You have free permission to do so, and it is in accordance with your nature. But perhaps this very holding back is the one suffering you could have avoided."

—Kafka

The RED Bandanna

PROLOGUE

THEY WAITED AT bedrock.

Seven stories below the ground, seventy feet deep in the earth, they sat. On a bright spring morning, while flags flew at half-staff in the memorial plaza far above, some seven hundred people had made the long descent to gather in this chamber. Together they met: strong and weak, mournful and hopeful, persistent and diminished. Families and firefighters, city officials and rescue workers, orphans and political leaders, they waited for the solemn ceremony to begin.

Shortly after ten thirty a.m., the president of the United States stepped to the lectern, dressed in a black suit and tie. He faced a cavernous room called Foundation Hall, a soaring open space with remnants of twisted steel and an exposed sixty-four-foot-high slurry wall, bolted in place as if it were still holding back the tidal waters of the nearby Hudson River. The president looked out at the numbered seats and ordered rows set up for the program, at the day's invited guests, including the governors of New York and New Jersey, the previous two mayors of New York City and the one currently holding the office, and a former president and his wife, who was the current secretary of state.

In this hole in the heart of a city, in a quiet and somber voice, Barack Obama began his speech for the occasion: the dedication ceremony of the National September 11 Memorial and Museum at ground zero.

As he delivered his first words, a mother sat backstage. After the president's remarks were finished, she would walk to a different microphone and share some of her family's story. For now, she sat out of sight of the assembly. There was a television monitor set up for her to watch the president's address, but she couldn't bear to look. Her eyes remained on the floor.

In the second row of seats, directly behind the mayor of New York City, a father kept his chin up and eyes forward, looking toward the podium. It was good that his wife would soon speak for him and their family. He couldn't yet bear to; the emotion would overwhelm him. As the president spoke, he sat and listened. At the first mention of his son's name, he began to weep.

President Obama speaking at the dedication of the National September 11 Memorial and Museum on May 15, 2014.

On September 11, 2001, in the worst terrorist attack in the history of America, 2,977 people died. Standing in the footprint of the fallen towers on that spring morning thirteen years later, the president chose to speak about just one. He singled out a young man who helped save people he didn't know in the South Tower of the World Trade Center before its collapse. He recounted the scene that had transpired in the 78th floor sky lobby. As fires burned and smoke filled the air, in darkness and chaos, a voice had risen, leading people toward the stairs and then down seventeen flights to safety. One victim had been too weak to make the descent, so he carried her across his back. When the young man had reached a lower floor with clear air, he'd urged the group to continue down. Then he'd left them, turned around, and climbed those long flights back up, looking for others he might rescue. For months, the man's identity remained a mystery, but one clue had emerged, the common thread of the descriptions of the people he'd guided and carried.

"They didn't know his name," the president told those assembled at the ceremony. "They didn't know where he came from. But they knew their lives had been saved by the man in the red bandanna."

The words echoed across the hall and off a graffiti-covered steel beam, standing tall in this part of the museum, a remnant of the towers. Amid the colorful messages and notes scrawled across the steel of the I-beam was a photo of the young man, a picture holding the promise that one day he would be found.

By the time Welles Crowther's body was recovered at ground zero in March 2002, six months after the towers collapsed, the truth was beginning to emerge. In the coming years, the inspiring story of his bravery and heroism and the fateful decision he made would spread, first from person to person and soon in newspapers, online, and on television. Welles made a selfless, fatal choice on that awful September morning. He was the man in the red bandanna.

ONE

WHENEVER WELLES WAS asked about his future, he had an immediate and confident answer: he would be a fireman. Not like the ones in children's books, but like the people in his family. From the time he was in preschool, both his grandfathers would take him to the firehouses in their respective towns in New York state—his mother's father, Frank, to the red-tiled, brick-faced, double-doored Fire Station No. 2 in Hartsdale; his dad's father, Bosley (whom the grandchildren called "Geeps"), to the firehouse in White Plains, just a few blocks from his house.

Welles also liked to spend time with Geeps in his home office, "playing business," as the boy called it, hiking himself up behind his grandfather's enormous desk in the sunroom, where

Welles, age four, with his fire truck.

Bosley would spend time writing. The interest in business would also last through most of his life. But it was an interest. Something to do. It wasn't firefighting.

The fireman's ideal was a magnet for Welles. The jubilant blast of the siren, the unpredictable call in the night, the monstrous gleam of the ladder truck, the fearsome power of the hose guns, the boots and turnouts and helmets, and the real and irresistible pull of fire—its brilliance and drama and danger. A living thing, a real and attacking beast. The appeal lay in all of it and something more, the chance to live out and execute an edict every child is taught but most forget fast: *you must help those in danger.*

On Christmas in 1981, when Welles was four, his grand-parents had a special gift for him, a blazing red ride-on fire truck. Upon first seeing it, Welles, who was formally dressed for the holiday in his little Eton suit, stood back for a few moments, as if uncertain how to proceed.

"He was afraid to go near it," his mother, Alison, said, picturing the scene. "He couldn't believe it was real. He was just so in awe of his fire truck."

The Crowther family lived in Pomona, New York. Their house on Ormian Drive had four bedrooms and a flat backyard of maybe half an acre backing up to a patch of woods.

One cold Sunday morning when Welles was seven years old, the family was getting dressed for church. They would soon be five: Mom; Dad, Jeff; Welles; his five-year-old sister, Honor; and the baby-girl-to-be, Paige.

With time dwindling and the church hour approaching, Welles called for his father's help. He was wearing a new suit, his first, gray flannel, warm and formal, Sunday best. Welles wanted to complete the ensemble by wearing a tie. But after a number of tries at tying it, he shouted down the hall, "Dad!"

Welles's father came, took a knee, flipped up his son's collar, and went to work. As he did, Welles looked down at his father, already dressed, and noticed a part of his wardrobe for the first time. He saw his father's pocket square sticking up in a few sharp points in perfect white spikes.

"What's that, Dad?"

"This?" he answered, looking down at his jacket pocket.

"Can I have one of those?"

"Sure."

After cinching the knot up toward the top button of Welles's shirt, his dad stood up and went back to his bedroom, looking for another white handkerchief. He kept a stash in his top drawer. He reached for one, and at the last second, anticipating where that clean white handkerchief might end up, he grabbed a second bit of cloth from his drawer before heading back down the hall to Welles.

When he returned, he bent down again and showed his son two handkerchiefs in his hands, one white, one red.

He took the white handkerchief and folded it into the same pattern as his own, with the points projecting upward, neat and sharp. He tucked it into the small breast pocket of Welles's suit coat and made sure the presentation matched his.

"Well," he said, "that's for show."

Then he pulled out the other handkerchief.

He looked at Welles and smiled, holding out a red bandanna. "This is for blow." He made a gesture, holding it up toward his face. "To blow your nose."

He made sure Welles understood the difference, and then

folded the red handkerchief neatly and placed it in the back right pocket of his son's pants. It was nearly identical to the blue bandanna he kept in his own back pocket.

"You can always keep this back there," he said. "You'll always have it if you need it."

"Thank you, Daddy," Welles said, beaming. "That's great."

During the service at Grace Episcopal, Welles stood straight, looked handsome, and felt proud. He was a portrait in his new suit. But it was the bandanna in his pocket, tucked inside with just the top edge peeking out, that gave his wardrobe that extra bit of flash, to carry and keep.

"Hey, Welles, do you want to come with me to the firehouse?" At eight years old, the answer was automatic.

"Yes, Daddy."

In the early 1980s the Crowthers had moved to Upper Nyack, New York, and by now, the town felt like home. Welles already knew many of the firemen as his father's friends, from seeing them at church or around town, but in this setting they possessed a different air. Larger, warmer, brighter in their blue T-shirts, they traded inside jokes punctuated by booms of laughter. They were a team. That team included Harry Wanamaker, Jr., a professional firefighter with the Fire Department of the City of New York. Harry volunteered his time with Nyack's

Empire Hook and Ladder and had a special place in his heart for Welles because he liked Welles's enthusiasm for the firehouse.

That day, the team of men was preparing for the upcoming town parade. For every firehouse in Nyack, the parade meant two things: an all-out war of pride in having the cleanest rig, and the tedious process of making it that way.

The volunteers wanted every piece of chrome blinding, every rim shining, every inch gleaming. The challenge for every ladder truck was the same: a lot of inches to cover, and a lot of them in places never meant to shine, or even to be reached.

When Welles and his father arrived, the men had started to remove the ladders from the bed atop the truck, and the space underneath was thick with leaves and sticks and congealed muck and grime.

Who was going to crawl in there? "Welles, you want to?"

The boy jumped right up to the top of the truck and crawled forward, his feet disappearing from view before being replaced by a set of hands sticking out from the top of the bed, waiting for the tools he'd need. He was handed a vacuum hose and began sucking out the detritus that the other cleanings and washings and waxings had missed. He was eager and happy. The men listened to the vacuum slurp and watched the hose stretch, and shared a hearty laugh. The kid was good. He was useful. Welles loved the feeling that he'd pleased his father, that he'd contributed, and that one day he would belong to the company and be called on to help, the same way the veterans were.

He was one of them.

~·◆ ◆·~

In a way, the firehouse was Welles's first team. There would be many others, with different uniforms on different fields. He poured himself into all of them, hearing the same mantras whatever the season.

Effort counts. Attitude matters. Hard work wins.

Before concentrating on hockey and then lacrosse exclusively, Welles played on Pop Warner football teams for several seasons, moving up each year by grade and weight. His lack of size became more conspicuous as the weight divisions grew wider, with a greater range of players competing against one another.

As one of the smaller ten- or eleven-year-olds in his grade, Welles played defensive back for the Valley Cottage Indians. He was the try-hard guy, the striver, the kid wringing out whatever ability he had through practice and will. A streak of fearlessness was useful too. Matt Drowne, a bigger teammate, remembered Welles's tenacity during drills vividly. "He was a genuinely tough kid," Drowne said.

He became part of a group called "the Mosquito Defense"— a bunch of light, quick players who took pride in being pests— persistent, annoying, buzzing around the ball. In their Pop

Warner league that year, the team went undefeated—and, to the great joy of the Mosquitoes, unscored upon—to win their league title.

Welles wanted a sleepover at the house to celebrate his eleventh birthday. About ten boys on a Friday night, eating pizza and watching movies, talking about sports and laughing at one another's fart jokes. What could go wrong?

Welles's dad smiled seeing his son's buddies coming through the door, from a few down the street who were a couple of years older to the brothers Dickie and Alexander Perry to longtime pals like Jon Hess. The smartest boy in the class, Jonathan Sperman, joined the gang for the night as well.

Welles's mom was away on a business trip, leaving his dad in charge. No heavy lifting. Have some pizza delivered, set out the snacks and soda, get a stack of VHS movies, and herd the boys downstairs into the finished basement—plenty of floor space to spread out the sleeping bags and blankets for the night. *Dragnet*, the 1987 movie with Tom Hanks and Dan Aykroyd, was selected as the featured film.

Welles's dad made his last check on the boys shortly after ten p.m., when the movie was just getting started. They were all settled in for the night.

Jeff slept soundly upstairs until snapping awake at nearly two a.m. He headed toward the basement to check on the sleeping boys.

The lights were all on; that was odd. He walked down the stairs. The sleeping bags and blankets were as empty as the room. No one was there.

Just then, he saw a prick of light out the windows looking over the deep backyard. Then another, and another. Small, weak beams were sweeping across the grass and into the trees, pointing in opposite directions. He rushed outside and heard the voices. The boys.

"Welles Crowther!" First and last name. Never good. "Get here *now*!"

Welles came across the yard to the back of the house.

"Dad, we were playing flashlight tag and . . ."

"Do you know what time it is?!"

Welles only knew that it was late.

"All you boys! In the house right away. Get inside and get downstairs . . ."

The boys came quickly, sweaty and flushed.

"Now," Jeff said, "get in those sleeping bags. Lights out immediately."

They bounded through the house and down to the basement and hopped in their sleeping bags.

Morning came, the boys left, and the episode went unmentioned until a few days later, when Welles came to his father, a pained look on his face.

"Dad," he began, "the other night during the sleepover, when you came out to the backyard . . . we didn't just play flashlight tag."

Welles explained. When his dad had found them in the backyard, the boys were actually returning from a bigger adventure. After the movie finished, someone suggested heading over to their old elementary school, where several temporary classrooms had been erected. The buildings were close to the boys' ultimate destination: the roof over the school's large all-purpose room, used as a gymnasium, auditorium, and lunchroom. Vast and flat, the roof held all kinds of treasures: all the lost tennis balls, baseballs, rubber balls, and footballs thrown across its space, collected up there, forgotten.

The roof was flat but more than two stories high, twenty-five feet up. It was used by the volunteers at Empire for ladder training. The boys found a route up using a walkway attached to the modular classrooms. One by one the boys made their way up, Welles near the back of the line, hesitant. Jonathan Sperman, the class brain, was last and refused to go, noting the danger and urging Welles to stay with him. Welles knew his friend was right, that it was foolish to go up, but all the other boys were already up, running around, scavenging for balls. Welles gave in and made the climb, leaving Jonathan behind.

Eventually they made their way down from the roof, across the schoolyard, and through the darkened streets to the Crowthers' backyard. That's when the game of flashlight tag had started.

Welles looked at his father, ashamed.

"What kind of punishment do you think you should get?" his dad asked.

Welles didn't hesitate. "No TV for two months," he said.

"How about two weeks instead?"

Relieved, Welles agreed.

As he entered middle school, many of the boys in his grade were a head and shoulders taller than Welles. He wasn't yet five feet tall. One bigger boy in particular used the bus rides with Welles to and from school to badger him. They'd board the bus near the bottom of Birchwood Avenue and North Midland in the village. A crossing guard stood sentry at the intersection, protecting the students in their comings and goings, but also serving as witness to their alliances and disputes.

It wasn't the crossing guard who called Welles's parents. It was the president of the PTA, a friend named Rikke Stone. Welles's mother was on the road, covering her territory in Long

Island as a saleswoman for an upscale women's clothing line, when she answered the call.

Apparently, Stone was driving up Birchwood, past the Crowthers' house, and saw two boys fighting on the front lawn. Well, it wasn't a fight, really. More like a pummeling, at least as Stone reported it. Welles was the boy throwing the blows.

"Pounding on him," Welles's mother heard from Stone. "Pound, pound, pound."

Welles's mom was baffled. She knew she needed to get home and talk to her son.

After getting back to Upper Nyack, she saw that Welles was unhurt, and in fact unmarked. He was calm.

"Welles," she asked, "what on earth happened? Who is this kid?"

"He swung at me with his lunch box," Welles said. "He was swinging at my head. So that's when I just took him down."

The crossing guard at the intersection would corroborate Welles's story. She had watched the tension building between the boys and described it to the school administrators.

"Mrs. Crowther," she said, "that boy picked on Welles every single day. Picked on him, tormented him."

Welles never spoke about any type of bullying with his mother at all, never betrayed that he was being picked on or harassed by another student. She knew her son well, and she knew his friends. But when asked, Welles told her plainly.

If there was any glint of pride in her, she hid it. She knew that Welles was doing what his father had instructed him to do. "Don't ever start a fight," he'd told his son years before. "But if one starts, be sure you finish it."

After finding out what happened, Welles's mom paid a visit to the boy's mother.

"You've got to get your son to stop this," she said. "He's got to stop picking on my son."

It was maternal instinct guiding her, but the intervention proved unnecessary. Welles had delivered the message on the front lawn with his fists, settling the matter. He would be picked on again as he continued through school, but not the same way, and never by the boy he'd felled on the front lawn.

Welles as a junior firefighter, at the Nyack town parade.

TWO

AT FIVE FEET two inches and just over a hundred pounds, Welles entered high school with a certain self-assurance—he was a good athlete, getting better, and a strong student on an honors track. Still, there were those who mocked him for his small size, sometimes good-naturedly and to his face, other times harshly and behind his back. He was different in ways easily spotted, even if he spent less time dwelling on the differences than others did.

One of the easiest targets was his wardrobe. In the early nineties, as the grunge scene took over suburban America, Nyack was no different. Ripped jeans and heavy flannels were the uniform of the day. Not for Welles.

Michael Barch, a classmate and buddy, remembered the style years later. "He was the opposite," Michael said. "L.L. Bean, Vineyard Vines. Nyack was old, grungy, plaid. Welles was wearing Polo shirts."

Keith O'Brien, who played hockey with Welles, remembered a time earlier when he got a new bag to carry all his gear—the skates, sticks, and pads that came along with the sport. The bags were massive, with handles large enough to slip over a player's shoulder, perfect as a prop to use in a prank where Welles was the target.

"We used to always make fun of Welles because he was so small," said Keith. "We bet Welles, 'I bet you can't fit in the bag.' So of course we got Welles to go into the hockey bag. Well, once you put him in the bag and zipped him up, what's the next thing you do?"

They looked to test the limits of the bag and its human cargo. "We lifted the bag and threw him down my stairs," Keith said. "I remember that he fit into the hockey bag, and once we got him in there we said, 'Okay, he is going down.'" Welles emerged unhurt and in good spirits.

Even his car was a target. It was a decidedly uncool van/box-truck contraption. The truck had its bumper torn off and a screeching backup safety beeper that emitted sound levels somehow higher and more shrill than a car alarm. Jody Steinglass, a classmate, remembered the echo and the mockery it inspired. "It beeped when you put it in reverse," he said. "When he pulled away from a party, it was *beep-beep-beep*. . . . I would've died if I had that car."

The vehicle was an endless source of derision, which Welles accepted and laughed at.

You don't play hockey, or drive through the dark freeze of winter mornings to watch it, because it's easy.

While other games require only an open field or a dirt diamond or a hoop on a pole, hockey needs more—a lot more, starting with ice. Sure, there are frozen ponds aplenty in Canada and Scandinavia, and more than a few in New England and Minnesota, and even some in Rockland County. But by and large around New York City's suburbs, the game is played indoors, on oval-shaped rinks in half-freezing warehouses.

There is no sunny side of the stands for spectators or shady dugouts to fill, no spring breezes to enjoy, only the stale cold air and the empty hum of the overhead fluorescents. For the vast majority of Americans, it will never be the game of choice. You don't play it by default. Skating is not just running. It's running across sheets of frost. The first fundamental is balance, and only after that's mastered does a player receive a stick, and then a puck on its end. The ice is a cold floor to receive your fall, and young players fall often and land hard.

Welles also played the easier games, but hockey held a special place for him. He was still undersized, but his coordination and effort lent him a quickness, a burst that served him and at times separated him from others. The game was physical and often reckless, with players crashing into the boards and one another, and the collisions gave the atmosphere a dash of chaos. From his first few games and practices, he was an elusive skater, able to navigate his way around traffic and avoid the big hits.

By his freshman year at Nyack High School, he was playing varsity, spending his time with the bigger boys, ready to compete in games. He played right wing—a glamour position, where a player earns looks at the net and chances to score if he flashes into the spaces where the puck is going to be.

Welles played smart and hard, his skill and speed developing. By the start of his junior year, he saw himself as a leader, but when coach Dave Moreno named the team's captains before the season, Welles wasn't chosen. Two other teammates, Matt Dickey and Chris Varmon, were selected. The same day, Welles sought out Moreno.

"Coach," he said, "can we talk about something?"

"Sure."

"I'm curious. I want to know what I'm doing wrong."

Coach Moreno understood immediately Welles was talking about the captaincy.

"What do I have to do?"

There were many ways for Coach Moreno to answer. Clearly, his player was disappointed, hurt, even. But Welles came to him directly, without sulking or taking an attitude or becoming a divisive presence in the locker room. The coach's answer was clear.

"It's not what you're doing wrong," he said. "It's just . . . there's more. You're a leader by example. But you can do much more."

"Okay," Welles said, turned around, and left.

His response came on the ice, in how he talked to other players, and in how he challenged other teammates in the locker room to care about each shift with the same intensity and effort, and to hold one another accountable when their effort flagged. The team's ultimate goal wasn't only to win but to move up the rungs of the league, to face greater competition.

Two weeks later, Coach Moreno called Welles in to see him.

He placed a large *C* on Welles's Nyack Indians jersey, naming him the team's third captain.

That year the team had 10 wins and 2 losses in league play, Welles turning a sharp wrist shot from the circle into a key weapon. He became known to the younger players as the veteran most willing to help them get their first goals for the Indians. When a player was still searching for the net, Welles asked Coach Moreno to put him on the newbie's line. Off the right wing, Welles would sweep in with a move to shoot, but then flip the puck across to a teammate he'd set up, having instructed him ahead of time to trail the play down the middle of the ice. When the play worked, the goalie was unable to adjust in time and change direction, and the teammate would redirect the pass into the net for his first career score. Welles would fly past, retrieve the puck, and bring it to the bench as a keepsake for his teammate.

His senior year, when the Indians played some of their games against League 1 opponents—the highest level of competition—the team finished with 6 wins, 5 losses, and 2 ties.

With the red bandanna tied around his head, worn beneath his helmet in every game, Welles was one of the section's leading scorers.

⌣⋅✦ ✦⋅⌢

Christmas morning, 1993.

Into the silence shrouding the house, the call came, indifferent to the gifts wrapped beneath the tree and the plans for church and feast and family, its shrill notes bleating out from the beeper.

Signal 10. Working fire. It was Welles's first fire call.

Two years earlier, Welles had finally asked the question his father had long awaited. He wanted to apply to become a junior firefighter, to start down the path toward joining him at Empire Hook and Ladder as more than a company mascot and ready hand. He wanted to answer the call. Welles was fourteen, still too young in his father's view. So he told Welles that he needed to be sixteen before he could apply and begin training. Two years later, shortly after his sixteenth birthday, Welles asked again. Dad agreed.

Welles had completed the county's firefighter training program that summer, learning the fundamentals of fire prevention and suppression, and spending time in the county's "smoke house," putting out supervised fires. He'd seen his father rush off to fires since he was a boy, and wanted to join him. This Christmas morning was his chance.

Welles had heard the beeper go off from his bedroom below and was dressed instantly. His father was out of bed, slipping pants on and looking for a shirt. He often slept with his socks on in case an alarm sounded overnight.

"Dad," he shouted up the stairs. "Better hurry up!"

Without a second glance they passed the tree and the spread of gifts beneath and pushed out the door. Welles's father flipped on the blue flashing lights on the dashboard of his truck and they made the turn to Empire. They were too late; the truck was already gone. The dispatcher sent out the call in more detail: a structure fire in Grand View-on-Hudson. Lights blinking, they raced to the address a little more than three miles south, directly on the river.

They caught sight of Empire's truck before getting there

and followed behind to the scene. The flames were plainly visible through the windows of the house.

Grand View-on-Hudson, a tiny village of less than a quarter of a square mile, was best known for its homes directly on the west bank of the Hudson River. The house on fire was more than a picturesque river cottage. It belonged to the most famous person in town, author Toni Morrison.

At sixty-two years old, she'd returned from Stockholm two weeks earlier after receiving the Nobel Prize in Literature. A giant of American letters, the author of *Song of Solomon*, *The Bluest Eye*, and *Jazz*, she'd won the Pulitzer Prize in 1988 for the novel *Beloved*.

Morrison wasn't at home. She spent most of her time an hour and a half south, living and teaching in Princeton as a professor of creative writing. The house in Grand View-on-Hudson was primarily a retreat, and a beautiful one. Now it was ablaze. Morrison's son Slade was alone in the house at the time the fire started, and according to police, he'd tried to react when an ember leaped from the fireplace and landed on a nearby couch, igniting it. He moved to tamp down the sparks, but quickly the flames mounted, growing out of control. He called the fire department, and within minutes, the four-story wooden Colonial was nearly engulfed.

They pulled up to a home overwhelmed by flames, drawing roughly a hundred firefighters to the scene. The two reported to the captain seeking instruction. Welles was dispatched with a third lieutenant to the side of the house, to assist with ventilation efforts. Welles's dad watched him walk to the edge of the riverside property and disappear. Whatever worries he had about his son crossing the bridge from training to task were meaningless now. Welles was on the line, in the company, answering the call, a responder. Besides, the father had his own assignment to handle in the front of the house as the fight wore on.

Slade escaped unhurt. The house, however, contained precious material. A portion of Toni Morrison's original manuscripts and other writings were inside, invaluable works of art. The firefighters understood that the priority was to extinguish and contain the flames, but, also urgently, to preserve the works and treasures of an American master.

Ultimately, the effort would last more than five hours before the fire was put down. A few of the firefighters sustained minor injuries. The house was gutted by the fire, but the manuscripts and writings survived intact. It helped that they'd been stored in a special study in the house, with some extra measure of fire protection.

Welles and his father crossed paths only once, during a water break, with the fire still alive. Likely they never saw the anxious homeowner at the edge of the property. After her son called her, Morrison had rushed north, arriving to see the final stages and the smoldering shell of her home.

The firefighters received the Signal 14. Return to quarters. When they got in the truck, Welles's dad looked over at him. "How you doing there?"

"Oh," he said. "I'm great."

The reply was redundant. As the truck pulled away, the smile through the grime was answer enough.

Lee Burns sat directly in front of Welles in Mr. Antonetti's twelfth-grade advanced English class. They were friends and fellow seniors, part of a group who congregated at the house of Karim Raoul, a classmate who had his own separate space on his father's property.

"We were always at Karim's," Lee said. "People would drink. . . . A lot of us were athletes who maybe had a beer, but we weren't smokers, we weren't into drugs. But there were kids around us who were into those things." Kids got drunk and got high, and sometimes got out of control and got themselves into trouble.

The high school had a self-appointed group to limit the damage. Varsity Athletes Against Substance Abuse, VAASA, was a collection of varsity athletes who pledged to be clean and sober. Some of the athletes in the group drank or smoked and used the extracurricular group to pad their college applications while flouting its mission. To their partying classmates, the group was sometimes viewed as preachy and laughable, the kids who wouldn't be invited to parties anyway but were somehow expected to provide an example to their cool counterparts.

Welles was invited to the parties, at least some of the time, but neither Lee nor others had ever seen him drink. Welles took his role with VAASA seriously and was the designated driver at every party he attended, according to his friends. Lee never heard him preach to anyone, or sound judgmental, but Welles spoke up when he thought he should. Burns had heard him often, and seen the eye rolls.

The best example he'd seen of Welles's self-imposed sense of duty came whenever there was a fire call.

There would be, Lee recalled, "the most beautiful girl sitting there," and then once Welles heard the fire call, "he's gone. We're having a good time, and that alarm goes off. He went to Superman mode and just went to the call."

One day at the end of English class, Lee, Welles, and the other students flooded out into the hallways, where Lee spotted his girlfriend, a junior, with another classmate, Wykeme Corker. The scene instantly upset him. The history between Lee and Wykeme wasn't good, and looking down the hallway, Lee believed Wykeme was bothering his girlfriend. In his mind, Wykeme, a sophomore football player, was a serial bully in the school.

Lee felt a rage building inside him as he saw Wykeme coming down the hall.

The floor was filled with students out of class standing at their lockers. Seeing Lee and Wykeme approach each other in the hallway, a crowd quickly began to form. They wanted a fight. Lee wasn't going to disappoint them.

"I was prepared to do whatever it took," he said.

There was no way for anyone to know what would happen if they charged at each other and tangled. Wykeme was a football player. Lee was six feet five and built. Neither was backing up.

Just then, Lee felt a hand on his shoulder and turned, hearing a voice in his ear.

It was Welles.

"Lee," he said. "Think of everything you have to lose."

Welles didn't talk to Wykeme. He spoke only to Lee. He was the only student to approach either one.

"I had this peace come over me," Lee said. "Almost immediately, I could feel my hands releasing, they weren't clenched anymore." Lee turned, found his girlfriend, and without waiting to hear what Wykeme was saying, he walked away. Welles stayed behind, watching them go.

❧ ✦ ✦ ❧

Even Welles's strong grades and high board scores and honor rolls and advanced classes and extracurriculars and varsity letters and captaincy, his work ethic and firefighting dedication and his family legacy and Division I lacrosse talent weren't enough for the Ivy League. Welles wasn't going to Princeton, as his grandfather Bosley had. Where his good friend Jon Hess was a freshman lacrosse player. Where he could pledge a dining club or give Toni Morrison a direct account of how he tried to save her house from burning down.

Instead, he was going to Boston College, a place he would quickly come to love and play for proudly.

Before going, Welles left behind that quintessential snapshot of a student's high school experience: the senior yearbook page. His stated ambition? "To make the best of everything, to sail around the world with the woman I love, and to paint my bumper."

Welles, proudly dressed in his lacrosse uniform at Boston College.

THREE

WHATEVER THE ARCHETYPAL college campus image, Boston College fills out the picture handsomely. Six miles west of downtown, the Chestnut Hill campus covers 175 acres, with more than 120 buildings and halls, draped across a hilltop overlooking its namesake reservoir.

The class of 1999, more than two thousand strong, arrived on campus in the late summer of 1995 feeling the way most freshmen do—high on autonomy, terrified of freedom, and hoping to fit in. There were mixers and orientation, academic registration and class sign-ups. And there were housing assignments, the single largest lottery piece in a student's arrival. A freshman dorm floor is a periodic table, a social experiment governed by forces not yet charted, the interactions impossible to forecast.

Welles was assigned to Duchesne East, not an ideal spot geographically. Duchesne East and West sit among a cluster of dorms on the Newton campus, separated from the heart of the college grounds, and typically requiring a shuttle ride to classes. It was widely seen as the worst of the freshmen spots to draw, and many there put in for housing transfers as quickly as they could, hoping to move to the lower, middle, or upper campus by second semester, to be closer to all things academic and so-cial. Welles wanted to move too, but understood he was stuck for the first semester, at least.

There was an advantage to having a precast identity to rely upon as an incoming freshman. In the first meetings and initial impressions and sizings up that formed the first few weeks of life in college, Welles had an answer to the question that came after *Where are you from?* He knew what he was into, and at any given moment, he was usually carrying the evidence. Welles came to Boston College to compete in Division I college lacrosse, the sport he loved most and played best. There were other pursuits, of course—earning a degree, finding a girlfriend, building a ramp to a career—but playing a sport at the highest college level was an immediate goal. Its demands would lend shape to his schedule, purpose to his days, and progress to the calendar. It would also provide a ready-made batch of friends. With sticks.

Johnny Howells, a classmate who would live with Welles in his senior year and become one of his closest friends, remembered the first several times he saw him across campus outside a quadrangle of dorms. Each time, Welles was carrying a lacrosse stick across his shoulder, twirling and spinning it by reflex, its webbing in constant rotation. Howells knew little about the sport but figured Welles for a good and speedy player, given his lack of size. Welles was still small, five six or five seven and barely 150 pounds.

If not dwarfed by many teammates as an incoming freshman, he was certainly in their shadows.

The Eagles' program wasn't a national power, but it was Division I. Welles's tenacity earned him the chance to continue playing. "Welles got it," said Ed Moy, his lacrosse coach at BC. "He considered it a privilege to play for the Eagles, even though he wasn't on scholarship or on the front page of *The Boston Globe*."

❦

Call it a very long pass, across fourteen years, from one lacrosse player to another. That's how Welles landed a summer job after his sophomore year at BC.

He was headed to Wall Street.

The internship at Sandler O'Neill, a small but powerful investment banking firm specializing in the financial sector, came from a hometown connection, Stacey Sennas McGowan, a managing director at Sandler. She was the president of her class all four years at Nyack High School, and after graduating in 1981, she went on to play varsity lacrosse as a team captain at Boston College.

When his mother asked Welles what he planned to do for the summer, he told her he was interested in finance. So she had a conversation with Stacey's mother, and shortly thereafter, Welles was on his way to apply for an internship.

At the interview, Welles was asked, "What would you say if I told you we weren't going to pay you anything this summer?"

"That's okay," he said. "The experience will really be worth it."

"Of course we are going to pay you," the interviewer said. "But I like your attitude."

Five days a week. Eight weeks. Each day he drove over the Tappan Zee Bridge to Tarrytown with his father. Together, they took the train to Grand Central Terminal, and from there, Welles caught the subway downtown. He liked it immediately, all of it: the firm was filled with characters, the city of Manhattan a throbbing buzz. The eight weeks flew by, and he made a good impression.

After six semesters and three lacrosse seasons at BC, Welles decided it was time to take a break. Not to relax, but to explore. Not on a different campus but another continent.

After spending his college summers working and hanging out in Boston and Cape Cod, New York City and Nyack, fulfilling the expectations of all around him—parents, coaches, friends—he found the chance to study abroad and break the pattern of school/sport/job thrilling. He'd be far from the firehouse and the lacrosse field, separated from those who already had his identity sketched and measured. It was a chance to draw a different picture and discover another self.

He'd talked some about studying abroad since arriving at BC. The school's summer Madrid program seemed the right opportunity.

Welles first met Chuck Platz at a program reception for American students in Madrid. A business student at Quinnipiac College in Connecticut, Chuck had already done a semester abroad in Madrid, where his family owned a small apartment, and decided to stay on through the summer, as part of an international summer program run by Syracuse University.

Most everyone in the group was dressed casually. Chuck, already accustomed to the culture, was dressed the way a typical Spaniard would have in 1998. "Jeans that were way too tight," he recalled, "with too many buttons."

Not Welles. He was in a navy blue Brooks Brothers suit and brown shoes, as if he were headed to a job interview or a board presentation after the reception. He was at once more formal and more forward than anyone else there.

The two hit it off immediately. They were matched up as interns and assigned to work together at Midland Gestion, an investment bank in the city. They spent their days learning the rudiments of financial research, how to evaluate companies. They reported to the president, Javier Carral Martinez, who met with the two young Americans without a set schedule and appeared to listen to them earnestly, or at least good-naturedly. In the evenings, they spent time in the ancient practices of the student abroad: pondering their future paths in the States and wondering where the next best nightlife stop might be.

Both shared the desire to find a job in New York City after graduating, preferably in finance. What that job would be mattered less than where. Manhattan was not the setting; it was the point.

All too soon, the program was ending.

Uncertain when they'd see each other again, Welles and Chuck downplayed their parting. Chuck was staying in Spain for another month, and Welles was returning to his last year in Chestnut Hill.

"I'm not really a fan of good-byes," Welles said. It wouldn't really be good-bye, as it later turned out.

For the more than eight thousand undergrads at BC there were over a dozen on-campus housing options—limestone halls or brick-faced dorms with names like Greycliff and Vanderslice, Thayer and Walsh, befitting the school's architectural aesthetic. "The Mods" didn't have the same ring to it, nor did they deserve it.

Originally constructed as modular housing, the rectangular-sided boxes had a strange appeal despite their unsightliness. They were coveted by students wanting the off-campus house party experience while still living on campus.

In the housing lottery, they were a prized pick for seniors of all stripes, and seemed to attract certain athletes in particular, like lacrosse players, and the friends of the players, and their friends a couple of times removed.

As for what the accommodations were like inside, one resident summed it up:

"They were . . . junky."

Six students shared the same unit in a Mod, which connected to another unit, for a total of twelve housemates. It was an unwieldy but useful number, large enough to be a force for chaos, a gathering in itself, but also a gang big enough to allow for factions and subsets. You could join in or break off, depending on your mood or agenda.

So it was for Welles and eleven others during their senior

year, living in the Mods units 22A and 22B: Chris Gangloff and Ben Gird, Justin Patnode and Robb Aumiller, Scott Dunn and George Leuchs, and the rest. George remembered the first time Welles made a clear impression on him. After getting the housing assignment at the end of their junior year, the group had already put together eleven guys, and over the summer still needed to find a twelfth. Someone mentioned Welles, known as a lacrosse player, familiar to some in the group but not all.

Welles planned to come by the off-campus house where a few of the guys were living, to talk. He came in, a sheepish look on his face, carrying a large car bumper.

"Um, does anybody own a car out front?" he asked. "Because . . ." Welles didn't finish the sentence. Just held up the bumper he'd sheared off trying to pull his van into the narrow driveway.

The owner turned out not to live in the house, which perhaps explained why Welles was unanimously accepted as the twelfth member of their senior Mod.

In each unit, the six mates were split into three bedrooms. Welles bunked with Johnny Howells. They'd met as freshmen, crossing paths in dorm hallways or at parties. Johnny, who'd grown up in Atlanta, was a Southern transplant, a rugby player. Not until the group formed in the Mod did any real bond grow. Quickly enough, they were friends—honest and close, needling and protective of each other.

"Just spending that much time," Johnny recalled, "getting to know him day in and day out, and getting to know his family, that's when I came to appreciate him."

But . . .

"There were definitely times when . . ." He paused, and spoke in the blunt tongue of a friend. "He was annoying."

The irritation usually came from spontaneity. Welles was rarely more than a few moments away from the next idea. *Let's grab the T. Let's head into the city. Let's go to Newport. Let's get a martini at a bar downtown.* Late Sunday mornings were ripe times for these suggestions. Johnny would roll his eyes and put his head under the pillow. *Come on, dude. Leave me alone.* Welles was rarely deterred.

Looking back on some of those irritating moments years later, Johnny had a different view.

"He always wanted to do more," he said. "I just look back and I'm like, I shouldn't have given him a hard time."

❧ ✦ ✦ ❧

In January 1999, during Welles's last semester of college, Massachusetts saw a stretch of fourteen consecutive days with higher-than-normal temperatures, peaking on the twenty-fourth at a balmy sixty-two degrees. At one point, there was rain followed by snow followed by rain followed by a sudden forty-degree plummet across Boston and much of New England, the drop coming in a matter of hours, before the melt could be absorbed back into the saturated ground. The result in the space around the Mods was a winter miracle.

The grassy courtyard between the buildings had completely frozen over, into a two-inch-thick sheet of ice. In one day, a perfect rink appeared outside the back door. It was a freak occurrence. It was a pedestrian danger. To a hockey player, it was an invitation.

But skating on the ice of an otherwise grassy yard was not adventure enough. To raise the stakes, Welles decided to take off his clothes, all the way down to the boxer shorts, the better to complete the scene. Out the back door he went, into a frigid midnight, gliding in easy loops and cutting crisp circles.

Johnny and a few others in the unit nearly fell down laughing at the sight. They also couldn't help but wonder how far Welles would be willing to go. One opened the door and called him over. Welles, skin red, smile bright, fog blowing out of his mouth, made a sharp stop near the door. The next step was obvious.

Bet you won't take the boxers off.

It was no easy maneuver in subfreezing temperatures to remove one's underwear while wearing blades on one's feet, but soon enough, Welles was buck naked.

By this time, the entire house was in an uproar, his friends falling over one another, wondering how long he could last. Then someone realized that it was a shame to deprive anyone in the Mods the sight.

"One of the guys started playing music," Johnny said, "to make more people watch." Slowly, heads started to peek out windows to investigate, and then to cheer and jeer the nude man in the hockey skates. Someone in the house flipped on the outdoor lights to improve the visibility, particularly for the women in houses across from the rink.

After skating across the slick space, after absorbing all the taunts and shouts, wondering if frostbite might be getting the better of him, he skated over to the back of the house. There was only one problem.

"Being good roommates," Johnny said, "we locked the door."

❧ ✦ ✦ ☙

On a splendid Monday in spring, May 24, 1999, Welles stood on the football field of Alumni Stadium with 2,139 of his fellow Boston College students, dressed in cap and gown. The class of 1999 was about to graduate, to turn its tassel and grasp its degree, to step away from the leafy campus in Chestnut Hill and into the wider world.

But Welles's father, high in the stands of the stadium,

Graduation day for Welles at Boston College, May 24, 1999.

couldn't find his son. All the young men and women stood far below, a dark monolith facing away from his lens. He wanted to see his son's face, and for his son to see his, to see his pride.

For such moments, when the father was in a crowd or at a distance and there was no easy way to get his son's attention, he'd developed a call the son would instantly recognize, a sound he'd respond to by instinct, no matter how loud or chaotic the circumstances. He started using the sound when Welles was just a boy, playing hockey or lacrosse or football, often to celebrate a goal, or a score, or a big play. Each time, Welles would look back or up or across toward his dad. It became a reflex. It was their code.

As he grew older, and his games became more competitive,

and the sports more serious, teammates would sometimes make fun of it, or ask if he ever wanted to tell his father to stop making the sound. But Welles never told his father, and he never asked him to stop.

So, from high up in the stadium now, trying to get his son's attention, he lowered the camera. All around, other families were yelling and shouting for their graduates, trying to make the same connection, to take the same picture.

The sound cut through all others like an arrow. Welles immediately heard and turned to face the stands. He smiled toward the sound and his father, and into the lens.

What the camera couldn't capture was the sound—the song of the code, the note that would always find its way to his son's ear.

It was the sound of a siren.

FOUR

WELLES STARTED AS a junior associate at Sandler O'Neill, the same firm where he'd been a summer intern, almost immediately after graduation. He was working at 2 World Trade Center. The South Tower. The 104th floor.

Twenty-two years old with a view to forever, or at least the sliver of forever glimpsed from the tower's windows, pinched between protruding columns on either side.

The dress code for the office was unwritten. This was finance. Wearing a suit was expected. And Welles did, happily.

But there was one part of Welles's personal dress code that would not be subject to office fashion. It was tucked in the back right pocket of every set of trousers and every pair of suit pants he wore every day. There were times when he would take it out, place it on his desk, and leave it there, though few noticed.

Natalie McIver did.

The assistant to the director of equity research at Sandler, she spent a lot of time with the firm's junior associates. Research was typically the first posting for those just joining the company.

Many of the junior associates wanted to leave research quickly after three or four months. They wanted to move to the rush of the trading desk, or the rewards of fixed income, or the prestige of mergers and acquisitions. Research, though essential, could feel like time in the salt mines.

Natalie sensed that Welles was different. While he might not be destined for a career as a research analyst, he didn't have the air of a man passing through or biding his time. The work was demanding, and that suited Welles just fine.

The hours were often long and stressful, but Welles showed little wear. Even in the busiest weeks, he kept his sense of wonder about where he worked, at the nerve center of the financial world, 1,126 feet up in the sky.

During one of the busier weeks, with everyone in the department juggling multiple reports and assignments, Natalie was surprised by a tap on her shoulder and a sudden introduction.

"Natalie," Welles said, "this is my dad."

He'd given no notice that his father would be visiting, or that he would be taking time out of the day to show him around the office. "None of us ever did that," she said. "Nobody ever brought their family through that I'd remembered. It was just so neat that he didn't take it for granted. I would meet my dad for lunch, but he would meet me downstairs. I never brought him around. I never thought of bringing him up."

Natalie watched as Welles guided his father through the office. The visit was short, but Welles made sure to show off the star attraction: the view from the narrow windows westward, where the research department faced, looking out over the Hudson and Jersey City, where Natalie lived, and beyond.

What struck Natalie too was Welles's ability to keep the job in perspective. His father's visit was one example; another was the red bandanna in his back pocket.

The first time she noticed it, Welles had taken it out and placed it on his desk. "What are you doing with that?" she asked. "I'm the one from Ohio. What are you doing carrying a bandanna?"

It became a source of ribbing whenever Welles took it out.

"What are you, a cowboy?"

"You forget this is New York? This isn't the South! Howdy do there, Welles?"

Welles would laugh and offer his own jabs right back, but the bandanna remained, either in his pocket or on his desk.

Most people in the office had no idea he carried it, or what its origins were. But those like Natalie, who worked close to him in those first few months at Sandler, recalled it clearly.

Whenever someone needed something extra done, said Natalie, some deadline beaten, some thorny issue solved, "Someone would just say, 'Hey, Welles, can you do . . . ?' Anything. Fill in the blank. 'Hey, you've got to solve this, fix this trade report . . .'"

In a dramatic gesture, Welles would reach for the bandanna on his desk or in his pocket, lift it above his head, and wave it in the air.

"He would say, 'This is where the magic comes from,'" Natalie recalled.

Other times—"I'm a superhero."

And once, facing some tall task, he lifted the bandanna, stood up from his chair, and made a preposterous declaration that Natalie never forgot.

"I'm going to save the world."

Rudy.

That's who came to Angelo Mangia's mind when he met Welles shortly after the firm's newest junior associate arrived at Sandler O'Neill. It likely wasn't a description Welles would've considered flattery.

Daniel Ruettiger was the "Rudy" to whom Angelo referred, the blue-collar son depicted in the beloved 1993 sports film of the same name. The movie tells the story of an undersized but scrappy kid who dreams of becoming a football player at Notre Dame but lacks the athletic talent and the grades to play for the storied Fighting Irish. Ultimately, he overcomes a series of obstacles (near poverty, dyslexia, meager physical gifts) to reach his triumphant moment—suiting up for the team, playing in a game, and getting carried off the field.

Welles was a much better athlete and a bigger physical specimen than Rudy; he'd grown to five ten or five eleven and filled out to 180 pounds by the time he left BC. He was a better student than Rudy too. But the managing director saw a bit of the underdog in the new associate, and sensed the same heart. "He wasn't the biggest guy," Angelo recalled. "He wasn't the loudest guy. He was just somebody thrilled to be a part of the team, who didn't shy away from anything."

As part of Sandler's culture, the more senior members of the staff were encouraged to act as mentors to those just arriving, to make certain they felt a part of the whole, and to nurture their talent in a way that would serve the company and the individual. Angelo, an attorney who helped to handle legal matters, relished the chance to be a big brother to some of the fresh faces.

Almost from the moment Welles walked through the doors on the 104th floor to begin a Wall Street career, he landed on

Angelo's radar, and the two hit it off. Why, exactly, was hard for him to pinpoint. Angelo was almost twenty years older, worked in a different area of the company, and was in a different stage of his life. He was also frustrated almost daily by the numbing commute from his home on Long Island to Lower Manhattan.

The two did share a love for the city's excitement, its events and restaurants, its juice and edge. In Welles, Angelo saw some shades of a younger self, and enjoyed being near that reflection—drawing off a young man's energy and guiding him through the beginnings of corporate life. There were dinners and ball games, inside jokes and late nights out. They quickly grew to be friends.

❧

"You've got to come up and see the office."

For Johnny Howells, the request was hardly a surprise. Knowing Welles since their freshman year at Boston College, living with him in the Mods in their senior year, Johnny had grown used to spur-of-the-moment ideas. He was visiting from Massachusetts. He liked coming to see his buddies who'd relocated to New York City, or as close as their paychecks could afford. For Welles, it was a shared basement apartment in Hoboken, New Jersey, a short train ride away.

It was a Sunday, and for most newly graduated from the soft schedule of college life to the grind of earning a living, the office was barely tolerable five days a week, if at all. Welles was already working more than fifty, even sixty, hours at Sandler O'Neill during the busiest times, and the weekends should've been a necessary relief, if not a complete disconnect. His love for the city, and for the office address in particular, was a magnet for him, though, especially with a friend in town. But Johnny also sensed a slight detachment as well. He liked that shade of dispassion; he saw in it a measure of humility.

"I don't know everybody that works on Wall Street," Johnny said. "But they think they're very important, and they're doing important work, and I never got that feeling about Welles. He wanted to make a good living, he wanted to live in the area, and why not?"

The two friends made their way to Lower Manhattan and Chambers Street. Without the press of commuters and clamor of the workweek, the atmosphere around the entire World Trade Center complex felt oddly still, as if on pause. The two entered the lobby of 2 World Trade and then took the elevator ride and transfer on the 78th floor before finally reaching the 104th floor of the South Tower.

Sandler's offices were deserted. The view was, of course, the reason to come, and together they absorbed the panorama through the narrow windows, the city's full scale laid out like a map beneath them. The sunny day's brilliance surrounded them on all sides. It was beautiful.

Welles took Johnny over to his area of the office, in research. His cubicle was perhaps ten feet from a window overlooking the East River, facing away from his apartment in New Jersey.

"Hey," he said, "take a look at this." He took out a glass from his desk, poured water into it, and placed it down on a flat surface. As winds hit the building, Johnny saw the water tremble and move, caught in the building's natural sway. Welles showed him how some of the office doors swayed slightly on their hinges as the building registered its gentle tremors. The structure was a living thing, beneath and around them, and Johnny could see the spell it cast on his friend, the pride he took in displaying its quirks of personality. This was why he wanted to make the trip. Not once during the tour could he remember him talking about the research, the reports, the job.

"I didn't get the impression that he was infatuated with what he was doing," Johnny said, "as much as where he was."

᠆᠆◆ ◆᠆᠆

It was a surprising offer.

Welles and Chuck Platz, his friend from the summer in Madrid, had spoken only a handful of times since they'd returned to the States, keeping vague tabs on each other's movements. There was little to prepare Chuck for the moment the phone rang.

"Hey," Welles said, as if they'd spent every other weekend hanging out. "Want to be roommates?"

It was the spring of 2000, and Welles was ready to move from Hoboken, and was seeking someone to join him, someone who had the same taste for city life that he did. Chuck was living with his aunt and uncle in Westchester, trying to save money, making the daily commute to his job at an asset management firm based on Park Avenue. The timing was perfect. The answer was easy. *Sure. Sounds great. Have you found a place yet?* Minor detail.

Welles and Chuck got a place fast, almost as soon as they started the search in earnest. They visited a spot in the West Village, just the second apartment they considered. Welles arrived first, checked it out, and headed back downstairs. Before Chuck even got inside for his own look, he saw Welles striding down the street toward him, a huge smile on his face. Chuck knew.

"Just seeing him," he said, "I said to myself, 'This is where we're going to live.'"

The apartment offered a view—if you stood next to the toilet, leaned hard against the wall, craned your neck upward out the top third of the bathroom window, and kept your balance, you might see a sliver of the upper reaches of the Empire State Building. That was north.

The view south was slightly less limiting, but through one of the bedroom windows, at just the right angle, you could see the peaks of two silver streams reaching skyward. A trip out the apartment door, down the hallway, and up two flights of stairs

Relaxing at the apartment on Washington Place in Manhattan's West Village.

to the roof of the building took them to a far more inspiring view. A mile south of the rooftop, piercing the horizon, drawing every eye: the soaring towers of the World Trade Center.

Not that Welles or Chuck made the trip to the roof daily, or even weekly. They were busy, immersed in the daily lives of young professionals in the city. But they never lost the feeling that they had scored: 115 Washington Place, prewar, downtown, two bedrooms, on the fifth floor, a mile from work.

For Welles, it felt destined. The apartment number was 19— his lucky number for as long as anyone could remember, the digits he wore on every jersey from the time he was a boy, the number he wore through his lacrosse career at Boston College.

They moved in on September 15, 2000.

"It was a stretch," Chuck said. "We were both young in our careers, so it took two of the four paychecks we got a month to pay the rent. But to this day, I would rent that place again in a heartbeat. If not for the memory."

Long days. Short years.

Time passed quickly outside the walls of apartment 19. The two men kept similar schedules, but with enough separation for each to have time in the pad by himself when he needed it. Typically Welles left for his day before Chuck did, and returned home first. Welles headed south to his spot on the 104th floor at Sandler. Chuck went northeast to his office in Midtown, in the Grace Building, across Forty-Second Street from Bryant Park. A few times a week after work, they made sure to meet at any number of city watering holes, typically back in the Village. A favorite was Boxers on West Fourth Street, a reliable bar and grill with cold beer and thick burgers, where they basked in their status as regulars.

During many of the weeknights out, they reminisced about their summer days together in Madrid, and wondered if there might be a way to relive them by creating a business that connected them to Spain. While they weren't exactly sure what services they might provide, or who their clients would be, or how such an idea would yield profits, they did have a name: Iberian Ventures.

"We thought of it as an opportunity for us to get back there," Chuck said.

While they chewed on the idea fitfully over the months, Welles also brought up another job, a much more radical departure from Sandler. Half a dozen times, at least, into the spring and summer of 2001, he raised the idea with Chuck.

"I'm thinking of taking the test," Welles said.

Chuck would look at his roommate and smile.

He understood how deeply rooted the notion was, reaching back to boyhood. Welles wasn't talking about the GRE or LSAT, some standardized assessment for graduate school.

"It was the exam," Chuck said, "to become a New York City fireman."

❧ ✦ ✦ ☙

On a summer evening in June 2001, Welles and his father climbed aboard the *John D. McKean*, one of the FDNY's Marine Company 1 fireboats, for a cruise around Manhattan's harbor. They were guests of Harry Wanamaker, Jr., the longtime volunteer for the Upper Nyack company who had once watched Welles scrub fire engines as a boy. Harry was a veteran of the FDNY and a member of Marine Company 1, New York City's first marine fire brigade. He'd invited members of the Empire Hook and Ladder Company No. 1 and the Nyack Fire Department for a tour.

"It was a beautiful evening," Welles's dad said. "We took some sandwiches and sodas and cruised around the harbor, around the Statue of Liberty, and back up the East River. We had a lovely time."

At one point, Welles's dad wondered where his son was. He hadn't seen him in a while, and wanted them to appreciate the city's twilight together. But Welles was nowhere in sight.

"I didn't see Welles for about an hour and then he popped up. I said, 'Hey, where you been?'"

"I was talking with one of the firefighters," Welles said.

"For an hour?"

Welles just smiled and looked out at the Hudson and the city shimmering in the fading light. He was enthralled by the moment: the setting, the camaraderie, and the conversation he'd just had with Tommy Sullivan, one of Marine 1's crew.

Tommy was ten years older than Welles, with thick black hair and a strong build. His first experiences on the river were working as a teenager in Stony Point, New York, scraping barnacles off boats. He'd joined the fire department seven years earlier.

That Welles would chat with Tommy was no surprise. He was endlessly curious, a natural conversation starter, and he already knew plenty of city firefighters from Empire Hook and Ladder, including Harry Wanamaker. What was unusual was that he didn't tell his father about what they'd discussed, at least not then.

Years later, Tommy remembered meeting Welles and his father, but the precise details of the conversation had faded. He knew both were volunteers at Empire and friends of Harry's, and recalled spending time with Welles and liking him. He surmised what he would have said when Welles asked his inevitable question about life with the FDNY.

What's it really like? How do you like it?

"I would've told him," Tommy said, "that I loved it."

It was the life he loved. There was no other purpose to match it, not the rush of the calls or the challenge of the rescues or the clarity of the mission. To serve.

As the boat coasted down the Hudson toward its home berth, Welles and his dad ended up side by side with Harry on the top deck.

"Welles, let me get a picture of you and Harry." He lifted the camera toward them as they moved together, shoulder to shoulder, Harry in his light blue uniform shirt with a black sash and radio handset across his chest. Welles stood beside him.

"Dad," he said, "make sure you get the Twin Towers in the background."

Jeff paused, years later, thinking back to that June night in 2001. "You can clearly see the World Trade Center towers off to the right of where they were standing."

Harry Wanamaker, Jr. and Welles on the deck of the John D. McKean *in June 2001.*

A few months later, in early August 2001, Welles made a call home.

The city was in the midst of a stifling stretch of summer heat and humidity, with temperatures in Central Park peaking at 104, baking the air. For anyone unable to escape to the Jersey shore or to the beaches on Long Island, the city was a hotbox.

Welles wasn't calling his father to talk about the weather.

After some small talk, he got to the point.

"Dad," he said, with a slight pause, "I think I want to change my career."

"Excuse me?" came the reply.

Welles had made the hard and prized move to Sandler's trading desk a few months before. He'd been with the company more than a year and a half, and was now in position to begin reaping serious rewards. For an equities trader at Sandler in the furious cycle of buying and selling, each day came with a scoreboard attached, based on the market's closing numbers. It was intense work, exhilarating at times, but exacting always; you didn't lightly step away from the game before the market closed and the scoreboard issued its tally.

Welles heard the note of incredulity in his father's voice. He expected it.

His father had spent his entire career in banking. He had many passions, to be sure, several of which he shared with his son. But a sound and secure profession came first, a career like the one Welles was beginning to build at Sandler. And it was a good career. Welles had already shown the ability to grow and be recognized. He'd made the leap from research to the trading desk. Sandler was a Wall Street finance player, and if one could withstand its pressures and endure its swings, it might well be a path to a lot of money. In years to come, six- and seven-figure bonuses and a bursting portfolio of his own. It was a chance at lasting, life-changing wealth.

"I think I want to be a New York City firefighter."

His father's mind immediately turned back to the June night with Marine 1, to Welles's disappearance for an hour, to his conversation with firefighter Tommy Sullivan.

"It's going to be four or five years, at least, before you could get picked up into the fire department."

"I understand that," Welles said. And then he outlined the most basic steps he'd have to take. He talked about the salary repercussions, the discipline he'd need. He'd already calculated how to finance the move.

"I figure I'll just keep working here," Welles said. "I'll save all my bonuses, and save as much money as I can, and then if I join the department, if I want to get married, I'll have a nice nest egg, I can buy a house."

He'd also pondered the time it would take him to reach the department.

"I'll keep going to the gym," he said. "You know I'll keep myself in good shape. I'll still be under thirty."

His father listened as Welles added one more point emphatically. "Dad, if I sit in front of this computer for the rest of my life," he said, "I'll go crazy."

Shortly after talking with his father in August, he began to explore the requirements for the FDNY.

The first was obvious. An application.

Even as he was thinking about becoming a firefighter, Welles progressed at his day job. He had made his way from the research to the trading side at Sandler O'Neill, and his friend and mentor Angelo Mangia could look out of his office and find his protégé just fifty feet away, at his desk, energized by the bedlam and frenzy.

"There's action going on," Angelo said. "I look over and in the midst of chaos, there's Welles, and he's just beaming. Always. He's thrilled. . . . He just really loved being at the firm and you could see it."

By the spring of 2001, Angelo's own time at the firm was ending, by his choice.

As he left the Twin Towers behind, he told Welles he wasn't going to be far away. He'd keep in touch. In the months that followed, he did. The two talked on the phone and exchanged e-mails regularly. "I would talk to Welles about how things were going at the firm," Angelo said. When they spoke, he heard something in Welles's voice.

"It was strange," he said. "I would say, in at least four of the conversations we had over the course of that summer, he would repeat the same thing to me."

Welles told him, "I don't know where I'm going to be. I just know I'm going to be part of something big."

As summer faded and Labor Day passed, Angelo checked in with Welles. He sent an e-mail. "How are you doing? Hope all is well."

The answer back struck Angelo. The e-mail was little more

than a fragment. "I'm okay, but a few words come to mind," Welles wrote. He listed the words in a terse column down the page:

Anxious.

Frustrated.

Aimless.

Bored.

Lobster.

Cold beer.

The coast of Maine.

Forever.

Welles.

Out.

"It was just very much out of character for him," Angelo said. "The words *anxious* and *Welles*, those were two words I would never use in the same sentence. You never saw him anxious. He didn't have that quality anywhere. Ever. So that gave me an uneasy feeling . . ."

The date of the message was Friday, September 7, 2001.

❧ ✦ ✦ ❧

The night of September 9, 2001, Welles was in the Village with his mom and dad. Welles saw his parents frequently, by his invitation. Compared with most twentysomething single men

```
Subj: well...
Date: Fri, 7 Sep 2001 3:00:56 PM Eastern Daylight Time
From: "Welles Crowther" <wrcrowther@hotmail.com>
To:   ajmangia1@aol.com

I'm okay, but a few words come to mind...
anxious
frustrated
aimless
bored
lobster
cold beer
the coast of maine
forever
welles
out
```

working in finance, living in an apartment in Greenwich Village, he was astoundingly open with his mother and father and eager to see them whenever he could.

They had made their way from Upper Nyack to have dinner with Welles and a few friends. Once dinner was finished, they would part ways.

Walking in front of his parents on the sidewalk, Welles reached into his back pocket for a comb to fix his hair.

"Welles, are you still carrying that thing?" his mother asked.

She wasn't talking about the comb. She was talking about the red bandanna wrapped around it. She couldn't remember the last time she'd actually seen him with it.

She laughed. "Here you are," she said. "Living in the city. Working on Wall Street. And you're still carrying around a red bandanna?" *Just like his father*, was the next thought in her head. Sure enough, he was carrying a blue bandanna in his back pocket, the way he always did. Red for Welles, blue for Dad.

"Of course I still carry it," Welles said, smiling.

And then, after combing his hair, he placed it back into the centerfold of the handkerchief, and put the bandanna back into his pocket.

To carry and keep, as he had for the last seventeen years.

FIVE

BLUE.

The sky that morning was an unforgettably brilliant shade of blue.

The night before, a cold front had pushed down from Canada and swept across parts of the East Coast, carrying rain and thunderstorms with it. Fresh cool air came behind, bringing unclouded skies the next dawn.

After the humidity and swelter of August, the morning was unseasonably cool, a gift to everyone stepping outside. Winds were gentle, and temperatures were in the low sixties at seven a.m. in the city, and predicted to climb no higher than seventy-five at the peak of the day.

The visibility was limitless.

September 11, 2001, was a perfect day for flying.

Welles's mother had slept terribly. On the night of September 10 she'd been struck by a wave of anxiety that came on with a force she'd never experienced. As she lay in bed trying to sleep, it was pushing her past worry, into panic. Getting out of bed, going downstairs, she tried to calm herself by writing her feelings out at the computer, but the screen appeared fragmented to her. She went back upstairs, into bed, and tried to go back to sleep. It was fruitless.

Up before six, she decided to go for an early morning workout at a fitness club. By seven a.m. she was driving across the Tappan Zee Bridge beneath the blue dome of sky.

Welles's father was going golfing. The bank where he worked had purchased the tee time in a benefit outing scheduled to begin later in the morning. It was the usual agenda. Breakfast. Pairings. Driving range. Drinks and prizes after the round. A good day for a man who didn't get enough days on the links. He was making his final preparations, getting ready to leave the house, when the phone rang. It was his older brother Bosley, calling from Virginia. "Hey, are you watching TV?"

＋ ＋

Jimmy Dunne, the managing partner at Sandler O'Neill, was already playing golf early that morning, to the surprise of no one who knew him. The night before, he'd told his mentor, Herman Sandler, that he wasn't coming into the office the next morning.

Jimmy was already on his sixth or seventh hole of the day when a man with a walkie-talkie approached him. The intrusion during a round was unusual for any golfer, and borderline heresy for Jimmy. Immediately, it drew his mind to worry if something had happened to his family.

"Are my kids okay? Is my wife okay?"

Yes.

Assuming the matter was not urgent, Jimmy turned back to the hole and played two more shots, until the man with the walkie-talkie grew insistent. "You need to call your office," he said. "Now. A plane hit your building."

＋ ＋

There were 14,154 people in the World Trade Center that morning. It was a city unto itself. The towers totaled 220 floors of Manhattan real estate. Each floor was nearly an acre of space—roughly equivalent to the size of a football field, all stacked on top of each other, separated by twelve feet of steel and a floor number.

They arrived from every direction, after grueling commutes on the Long Island Expressway and traffic clogs in the Holland Tunnel, by the lettered and numbered lines of the subway, in the PATH trains from New Jersey sliding beneath the Hudson, and on the Staten Island Ferry churning across the water, out of the gridlocked streets east of the Battery, and out of cabs that stopped along West Street.

Welles left his apartment on Washington Place in the West Village around seven that morning, as he usually did, his suit and tie straight out of the cleaner's plastic. From the time he started at Sandler, he liked to arrive at the office early to get a jump on the day, for the impression it created, and for the savings. The firm often served a great breakfast spread, and Welles didn't like to miss out.

It was little more than a mile and a half from his door to the entrances of 2 World Trade, his tower.

When Chuck Platz woke up on the morning of September 11, Welles had already left the apartment. Chuck's bedroom was next to the bathroom, and often he heard the sounds of his roommate's morning rituals, the shower and shave that started his day. In this regard, Welles was considerate, down to the detail of often waiting to put his shoes on only after leaving the apartment, to minimize the noise.

The first signal came more than an hour after Welles had closed the door, when Chuck was in the bathroom. He was standing at the sink, shaving, when he heard a sound that shook the bones of the room itself, rattling the glass in the mirror, a roar that forced him to tense his upper body, as if bracing for a blow.

Trying to follow the sound, Chuck left the bathroom, walked into the bedroom, and looked south from the window. As he had done so many times before, he found the spot that granted the best vantage of the Trade Center. He saw the tops of the towers. One of them was on fire.

He rushed to get dressed and headed down the five flights out the entryway of the building and onto the street. The first person who spoke to him was a crossing guard for the Academy of St. Joseph, an elementary school next to the apartment building. He could hear others already talking about a bomb going off downtown, or accounts of a small plane hitting one of the towers, but the guard, still looking skyward, was definitive.

"That wasn't a bomb," she said. "It was a big plane."

Time stood still there on Washington Place as Chuck stared up at the burning hole on the face of the North Tower, like so many others around him. The sight was at once vivid and impossible, a vision beyond comprehension.

His mind cleared with a single name: Welles.

Natalie McIver was tired. She was seven months pregnant, and for the past two and a half weeks she'd been working without one of her key colleagues by her side. Despite Natalie's intention to be in early that day, her body argued for another hour of sleep. After getting up and out of the apartment in Jersey City, almost directly across the Hudson from the Trade Center, she made the walk to the ferry for the ride across the river. She stepped on the ferry, taking in the magnificence of the day. While still on the water, she heard a strange thunder in the blue sky.

She looked up, and saw the plane. It was very low.

Ling Young was walking across familiar ground. She was an auditor for the New York State Department of Taxation and Finance, an agency that claimed space on the 86th and 87th floors of the South Tower.

Ling's work was primarily out in the field, but today she was coming in and heading up to the 86th floor.

At forty-nine years old, she still found her trips to the Trade Center vaguely exciting, the complex buzzing with humanity, so many lives crossing in its concourses and open spaces. Her only apprehension, if there was any, was rooted in the 1993 terrorist attack there. She was grateful not to have been in the towers that February day, but the terror still registered with her, if dimly, when she reported to 2 World Trade.

Ling reached her office before eight a.m. Less than an hour later, she was talking with a supervisor when their conversation broke off in midsentence. Each looked at the other, startled into silence. She swore the sound was an explosion.

Judy Wein had gotten in earlier than Ling Young and was stationed higher in the building. Judy, forty-five years old, was a senior vice president at Aon Corporation. That September morning, she commuted in from Queens with her husband, Gerry Sussman, as they did most workdays. After getting to Lower Manhattan, the couple walked together to City Hall and stopped to kiss each other good-bye. Judy went off to her corner office on the 103rd floor of 2 World Trade. Her view faced west, out over the Hudson to New Jersey, and on a day this clear, seemingly beyond. Toward the north, a part of 1 World Trade blocked a stretch of horizon. She ate breakfast in the office, a plate of yogurt and fruit, and began to work. About an hour and a half after she arrived, she heard a massive boom right outside the window.

She looked up instantly in its direction.

That's when she saw the enormous ball of fire rising from below.

Eighty-three people were in the offices at Sandler O'Neill that morning readying for meetings and reports, trades and positions, the e-mails and calls that would shape the nine or ten hours ahead.

Impact.

8:46:40 a.m.

American Airlines Flight 11 out of Boston, a Boeing 767 jet with eighty-one passengers and eleven crew aboard, was carrying 10,000 gallons of fuel and traveling at 465 miles per hour when it crashed into the North Tower of the World Trade Center.

The jet slammed into the north side of the building, killing all ninety-two on board as it exploded through seven floors of the tower. It measured 156 feet across its wingspan, the jet's left tip blasting through the 93rd floor, while its right ripped through the 99th. The path of destruction ran directly through the offices of a single corporation, the Marsh & McLennan Companies.

The force of the crash was so great, parts of the plane's landing gear burst out the south side of the tower, opposite where the plane entered, flying the length of five city blocks through the air before landing in the street. The plane's fuel ignited on impact with the building, triggering an explosive fire.

Chuck Platz's photo of the Twin Towers the morning of September 11, 2001, taken from the roof of the Washington Place apartment building.

Chuck Platz reached for his phone. The call went straight to voice mail. He tried again. Same.

His next impulse was simple: Go. Go there. Get to him. Get on the subway and head south to Chambers Street, up and out to the plaza, to find a way to reach Welles. Or walk or run there, through the chaos. He didn't stop to calculate whether the smoke he saw in the moment was pouring from the tower closer to him or farther away, whether it was World Trade Center 1 or 2, the North Tower or the South.

He headed toward the subway, but downtown service was already being suspended. He turned around and headed back to 115 Washington.

If he heard the second plane hit, or understood that its target was the South Tower, Chuck can only recall walking into the building and making his way upward, past the apartment on the fifth floor, until he reached the roof. The smoke from the towers was flooding outward now and blurring the city's skyline before his eyes. He continued to call Welles, without success. At one point, he left a message, forcing himself to sound casual and matter-of-fact. "Hey, make sure you're okay. I'll meet you at Boxers tonight."

A short time later, standing in the same spot, he saw the first tower fall. He didn't know whether it was the North or the South Tower, the one where Welles worked or the one he looked at from his 104th floor office. Chuck was paralyzed by what he saw and couldn't understand, what he feared and didn't know. "People asked me if, in my heart of hearts, I knew," Chuck said. "My mind wouldn't allow itself to form a thought."

Something primal kept his rising panic at bay: hope.

Only 131 feet separated the towers—less than half a football field of open space between a furnace of flame erupting from the gashes of one structure and the gleaming façade of the other.

Inside the South Tower, people on the highest floors facing west could feel the extreme heat through their office windows.

In the first several minutes after Flight 11 hit the North Tower, confusion ruled everywhere, including in the South Tower, where even those facing away from the plane's entry point felt the reverberations of the crash. Many who could see the damage assumed that a small plane or helicopter had flown into the building. The smoke made it hard to absorb the scope of the devastation.

In her office at Sandler O'Neill, on the 104th floor of the South Tower, Karen Fishman was talking with Gordon Aamoth about a deal he was working on when she heard Herman Sandler, and perhaps Chris Quackenbush as well, two of the firm's three leaders, make the announcement that a plane had hit the North Tower.

She ran out of her office into Quackenbush's to see what had happened. A truly panoramic view wasn't possible in the towers, particularly up close. Its windows were less than two feet wide, just eighteen inches across. The towers' architect, Minoru Yamasaki, suffered from a fear of heights. The narrow office windows, with pillars on either side, restricted the views. Karen's view from the windows in Chris Quackenbush's office was complicated by a storm of paper blowing through the air and a growing cloud of smoke.

Mark Fitzgibbon had been Welles's boss on the research side of Sandler until Welles moved to the trading desk. He was in his office that morning, meeting with his colleague John Kline, both of them oblivious to anything happening outside, when the two heard a commotion outside the door. The office was next to a stairwell leading out of Sandler's offices. Opening the door, he smelled what he believed were the first few wisps of smoke. He saw a few people quickly moving toward the stairs, and assumed it was a fire.

Herman Sandler tried to be clear and calm in the instructions he gave to all in the office this morning. They had not been given any official evacuation order yet. No one had to leave. But anyone who felt uncomfortable at all and wanted to leave should absolutely go.

On the 104th floor, some had a sense or made a choice before or after hearing Herman Sandler issue his instructions. Already, they were making their way toward the elevators or into the stairwell near Mark Fitzgibbon's office.

✦ ✦

Before nine a.m., Welles was at his desk when the phone rang. It was his friend and former roommate Johnny Howells. Johnny was in Boston, at work in his home office. Minutes earlier he'd been on a conference call when his housemate interrupted to tell him a plane had hit the World Trade Center. Howells muted the line, looked to the television, and saw smoke pouring from one of the buildings.

He got back on the line, telling others on the call he had a friend working in the towers. He had to go. Despite the visit he'd made with Welles to the offices at Sandler on that quiet Sunday afternoon a year before, when Welles was so proud to show off the views from the 104th floor, Johnny couldn't remember which tower they visited. Where was the office? Was it the North Tower or the South? Where was Welles right now?

He picked up the phone and, still watching the dark clouds surging out of the building on his television screen, dialed Welles's desk number. Almost immediately, Welles answered.

"Welles," Johnny said, "are you all right?"

"Yeah, I'm fine," Welles replied. His voice was clear. "It was the other building."

"Get out of there," Johnny said, without hesitating.

"I think we're okay," Welles answered. If there was any edge in his voice, Howells didn't hear it. "Something hit the other building. You could feel it, but I'm all right."

Johnny, along with millions of others across the country and around the world, was seeing the first images of the devastation to the North Tower, the first seeds of catastrophe unfolding in real time in their living rooms and kitchens and offices.

But Welles was 131 feet away from the burning North Tower and had only a vague sense of its condition.

Johnny repeated himself, more forcefully this time. "Get out of there."

"Actually, they're coming on now," Welles said, referring to an announcement being made over the office speakers. "They're saying we are going to get out of here so . . . I'll give you a call later." The call ended there.

It was 9:02 a.m.

Through the South Tower's PA speakers, the Port Authority broadcast the message:

"May I have your attention, please. Repeating this message: the situation occurred in Building 1. If the conditions warrant on your floor, you may wish to start an orderly evacuation."

One minute later.

9:03:02 a.m.

United Airlines Flight 175, another Boeing 767 jet out of Boston, flying northward at a speed estimated between 540 and 590 miles per hour, losing altitude at a rate of 5,000 feet per minute during its final nosedive, banked at the last second before slamming into the South Tower.

The plane, carrying a nearly full load of 10,000 gallons of fuel, tilted its left wing down just as it hurled itself into the building. The wings sliced through seven floors of the tower at the initial crash point, the impact zone running from the 78th to the 84th floors. Upon hitting the façade, its jet fuel ignited, spreading across space, bursting into savage fires and sending out waves of broiling heat.

The entire tower rocked with the force of the crash, shaking from its top floor down to its foundation and below, pulsing into the bedrock. The building pitched hard in one direction before its steel core bent back the other way, swaying violently from side to side.

The plane's nose crashed into the 81st floor at the first point of impact, a place in the tower holding a concentration of heavy elevator machinery. The fuselage rapidly disintegrated as it plowed into the machinery's immense bulk. Through most of the building, the three main stairwells were bunched close to one another, and close to the building's center. Here, in the impact zone, the stairwells were spread out, closer to the edges of the tower, to make room for the hulking elevator machinery, which took up so much space on these floors.

As a result, Stairway A, the stairwell in the northwest corner of the tower, farthest from where the plane entered the building, withstood the devastating effects of the crash. It remained intact.

These stairs were the sole path down.

꒰｡･◆ ◆｡꒱

Mark Fitzgibbon, John Kline, and Karen Fishman were already well on their way down that stairwell. After the first plane hit the North Tower, each made the decision to leave quickly. Mark hesitated for a moment, but saw Karen in the hallway, and she urged him to go. She also told him not to take the elevator. She remembered people being stuck inside the cars for hours, having to be discovered and freed during the 1993 attack.

If Stephen Joseph, Jace Day, and Andy Cott shared Karen's misgivings about the elevators, they ignored them. Stephen Joseph, a Harvard graduate and Vietnam veteran, heard the echo of his military training: in a crisis, get to a position of safety first. Only there can you best evaluate the threat and be in position to react and respond. Less than ten minutes after Flight 11 struck the North Tower, he and his colleagues stepped into an elevator outside Sandler's offices and went directly down to the sky lobby on the 78th floor.

Stepping off, they looked to transfer to a different bank of cars heading the rest of the way down to the ground floor. The elevators were enormous, the size of a room, with enough space to fit fifty-five people. The cars were designed to cover the seventy-eight floors down to street level, 844 vertical feet, in less than a minute. The first elevator was full. They moved to another car, which quickly filled up as they stepped inside, and went directly down to the tower's lobby. More than sixty floors above, Karen and Mark were continuing to make their descent through Stairway A. The stairwell was growing more crowded, but the atmosphere wasn't edgy or panicked. Karen also saw a smaller group of civilians, office workers who were climbing back up. They had reversed course from their descent. Likely, some had heard the Port Authority's announcement at 8:55 a.m. instructing tenants to remain in the building:

"Your attention, please, ladies and gentlemen. Building 2 is secure. There is no need to evacuate Building 2. If you are in the midst of evacuation, you may use the reentry doors and the elevators to return to your office. Repeat. Building 2 is secure."

On the 68th floor, Karen saw a fire marshal echoing the message, telling people in the stairwell it was safe to go back upstairs. The incident was confined to the other tower. She paused for a moment, then disregarded the instruction, walking past him and continuing downward.

She was just a few floors farther down when Flight 175 slammed into the South Tower. Sixteen minutes had passed since the first plane struck the North Tower. Mark Fitzgibbon, also in the stairwell, was immediately thrown from his feet as the building shook from side to side. He could sense the entire structure around him rocking back and forth, and briefly wondered if the tower could stand. Eventually, he found his way back to his feet and, along with the others around him, regained his bearings and began moving down the flights as fast as he could, with urgency now, taking the steps three and four at a time.

John Kline was also moving as quickly as he could, now understanding with a terrible clarity that the buildings were under attack. Even as he gained ground, moving closer to the ground-floor lobby with each step, the stairwells were growing more crowded, the pace slowing, the line backing up, and people pressing into one another.

Soon, he, Stephen Joseph, and Karen would reach the lobby, and despite the debris raining down from the skies outside, they would push forward to safety. They didn't know it, but they were no longer just part of Sandler's eighty-three, the number of people who were in the office that day; they'd joined a very different group, the seventeen who survived.

There was no obvious note of panic in Welles's voice as he left a message with his father's secretary to assure him he was all right. He knew his dad would certainly check in upon hearing about the plane crash, and he'd have the message waiting. Next, he called his mother on her cell phone.

She never heard the call, and it went straight to voice mail. Welles left a short message.

"Mom . . . this is Welles. I . . . I want you to know that I'm okay."

The time was 9:12 a.m. They were the last words his family would ever hear him speak.

Soon after hearing the boom from the first plane striking the North Tower, Ling Young felt heat penetrating the department offices on the 86th floor of the South Tower. She didn't know what had happened, but feeling the heat was enough. She and others around her made the decision to leave.

The small group got in an elevator on 86, heading down to the sky lobby on the 78th floor, for the transfer to the express elevators to the ground-floor lobby. Crowded with people just arriving for the day's work, the area held perhaps a hundred or more ready to switch to local elevators for the upper floors, and others, like Ling, looking to go back down.

There were no cars open for the trip down. Ling's group waited among the larger crowd, and began to talk. Like everyone in the lobby, they were stalled there, suspended between going up and coming down. Some of her colleagues were trying to figure out the cause of the explosion in the North Tower. No one knew for sure. One suggested going back up to 86, to see if they might call the governor's office for more information. They also heard the announcement over the building's PA system telling people to return to their offices, as the incident was confined to the other tower. Ling was firm. The burning smell was growing a bit stronger, faintly like burned rubber, or at least that was the sense she had. She was going down.

An elevator appeared, its doors opening. As she and the

others stepped toward it, the wing of Flight 175 burst through the wall. The lobby exploded.

The impact threw Ling from one end of the elevator lobby to the other. Unsure if she'd ever lost consciousness, she lay on the floor nearly smothered in dust and debris for what felt like minutes before even trying to sit up. Fires burned a small distance away, in the middle of the lobby, and flames were shooting out from the elevator shafts. The walls and ceiling of the lobby had been vaporized, and huge banks of windows shattered.

Moments earlier, she had been waiting to board the open elevator, hearing conversations echo through the lobby. Now many of those lives were silenced. She was surrounded by people who were dead and dying.

Ling gazed down at her body. She was injured and badly burned, but she felt no pain, the hurt smothered by shock. She sat where she was, on a portion of the floor still intact, uncertain what to do. She worried that if she moved, the entire floor would collapse beneath her. She heard sounds, signs of life, and understood she wasn't alone. There were others around her, colleagues from her office, all badly injured. No one moved.

Ling Young stayed still for what she believed was ten minutes, perhaps longer, paralyzed by fear. Then she heard a voice calling out, clear and strong. Instantly she turned toward the sound. "I found the stairs," the voice said. "Follow me. Only help the ones that you can help. And follow me."

For the first time, Ling stood up. She moved toward where the man had called from and finally saw him.

"It was a young man," she recalled a decade later. "Not very husky. Very short hair." She remembered that he was white, wearing a white T-shirt, and appeared to be uninjured. She thought she saw him with a red bandanna.

"That image has stuck with me," she said. "Almost on a daily basis, that image has stuck with me.

"A bunch of us just picked ourselves up and followed him right to the stairs."

Ling couldn't tell how many were with her as she entered the stairwell. The smoke and dust on the floor persisted. She moved forward slowly, struggling to walk, holding her arms out in front to steady herself. As she walked, she noticed a white man behind her whom she described as tall and thin. She didn't know who he was. The man who steered her toward the stairwell was also with the group, walking behind her, urging her to move forward and not to stop.

They continued down the flights of stairs until the air began gradually to clear, the smoke dissipating. At one point, Ling turned to see the young man behind her, the one who'd led her to the stairs, and for the first time she noticed he wasn't alone. He was carrying someone over his shoulder as he walked down.

"It was a very light-skinned black woman," Ling recalled. "She was tall. He was holding her across his back." Ling didn't know who the woman was, only that the man had apparently been carrying her the entire way down since leaving the 78th floor.

They reached what Ling believed was the 61st floor, and then the man stopped. He lifted the woman from his shoulder and carefully put her down on the stairs. She sat down immediately. Ling looked at the man. She remembered thinking that he had a baby face.

The man asked Ling to take the fire extinguisher he'd also been carrying. It looked heavy, impossible, but she lifted it. He urged her and the woman sitting on the stair to continue downward. Then he reversed course.

"I'm going back up," he said.

Ling understood at once what he meant. He was going back to the 78th floor, seventeen flights. He was going back to the sky lobby. The man turned and, without saying another word, left her behind.

Ling Young exhorted the woman beside her to get up and keep going down. To move even a single step at a time. The woman said she couldn't. Ling left her, carrying the fire extinguisher the man had given her for a short distance, uncertain where she found the strength, before setting it down. She walked carefully, her pace slowing, until she encountered an FDNY fire marshal, Jim Devery, near the 51st floor.

"She had her arms out. Her eyes were nearly closed," Devery said. "I couldn't leave her there."

He reached out and picked up Ling, carrying her as best he could down the next ten flights. Devery couldn't remember her saying anything as they climbed down. When they reached the 40th floor, exhausted, a fireman opened a door to the stairwell, asking if they needed an elevator. They left the stairs and followed the fireman into a service elevator that was still working. Seconds later, they were on the ground floor.

Devery wanted to get Ling to triage, or to an ambulance, to get her medical care as soon as he could. He took Ling out toward Vesey Street, and eventually placed her in an ambulance.

꜠✦✦꜡

Judy Wein, the executive from Aon Corporation, had also been in the sky lobby when it exploded. Badly hurt, Judy scanned the lobby, desperately searching for a way out. That's when she heard a voice and saw a man wearing a red bandanna. He was pointing people to the stairs and telling them he'd found a route to safety.

Judy stood up, walked toward the man, and followed him into the stairwell. It was brighter there, and he pointed the way down. She began the long trip down seventy-eight flights of stairs, with others behind her. Somehow, the group made it to the ground floor and out of the building. Judy was placed inside an ambulance with a Chinese woman. The woman was caked in dirt and clearly in shock. Judy didn't know her name. She'd never seen her before. It was Ling Young.

The ambulance carrying them pulled away. Moments later, the two women heard a fearsome roar. They turned to look out the back window.

The South Tower was falling.

Fifty-six minutes after Flight 175 hit the South Tower.

9:59 a.m.

Collapse.

The South Tower's disintegration took ten seconds.

It took ten seconds for the tower's 750 million tons of heavy steel and concrete to drop, erased from the skyline. The energy released was an enormous bomb, creating dust storms and debris fields. Nearly all matter within and beneath the tower was crushed flat in those ten seconds, driven down fifty, sixty, seventy feet beneath the street.

After reaching his family as quickly as he could to let them know he was safe, Chuck drifted through much of the rest of the day, unable to shake off the paralysis that so many felt, not only in the city but across the country and the world. For hours, his gaze shifted back and forth between the images playing on the television and the smoke from downtown drifting outside the bedroom windows. The calls he made went unanswered, the door to the apartment stayed shut.

As night fell, he left the apartment and went to the only place he could think of, guided as much by routine as by the hopeful message he'd left earlier in the morning.

He sat in the bar at Boxers for hours. Every time he heard the door open, he looked to see if it was Welles. Finally the owner, offering his apologies, said he needed to leave. It was time to close.

Welles's parents and sisters, aunts and uncles, college buddies and teammates, fellow firefighters and childhood friends, all the circles of his life, they all waited, holding back their grief.

SIX

THE NEXT DAY, Wednesday, September 12, Chuck Platz breathed deeply, paused, and walked into Welles's bedroom for the first time. Chuck was twenty-three years old. The most significant loss he'd experienced in his life was the death of his grandfather when he was seven. No one else he'd known well had died.

He looked down at the threshold, the saddle of wood on the floor between the hallway and the room. He paused.

Outside, where streets had been blocked off and an emergency force mobilized, where a smoldering pile complicated by bodies rose 150 feet in the air, where the small city of the Twin Towers had populated the sky a day before, where families and friends were beginning to post signs of their missing loved ones on every flat surface they could find, there were millions of souls all grappling, alone and together, with anger and pain, doubt and fear.

Inside apartment 19, there was stillness.

The glass of water was still on the dresser.

The dry cleaning receipts for Welles's suits were still pinned underneath a wooden loon, the one he used as a paperweight.

The dent from Welles's head was still in the pillow.

In the silence, Chuck heard the first echoes of his friend's life. Nothing definite had emerged as to his fate, no authority had decreed his end, no official had called or come by. But in his heart, Chuck knew.

He could hear Welles walking out the door, the sound forever tracked in his mind. The vacancy of Welles's room would stay with him for years to come.

"Even today, I take a second to look around my room when I'm leaving for the day," he said more than a decade later. "To maybe tidy up the bed or clean things up. Not that I'm thinking I'm not coming back, but it's just this little reminder, in the back of my head, of what it was like to walk into his room, of what it looked like, just the way it was when he walked out the door that day.

"I find myself doing little things like closing the closet door, fixing up the bed, putting the remote on the back table. . . . I feel like I'm doing them because of the memory of walking into his room and seeing it like he just left it. He left as if he was coming back. . . . It was hard to see. So I think maybe in some ways, I try to make it look neat when I leave my place. For him."

Welles's father was the one who went to the city to search, to fill out the forms and answer the questions. The morning after the attacks, he woke up early to ride in with his friend Tom Weekley. Jeff brought documents with Welles's fingerprints with him. He also went to the family dentist to collect his son's dental records.

He joined a march of loved ones bearing the open wounds of their panic. Maybe it was natural that families of the missing turned to a fortress in the city, a place meant to symbolize security.

The armory on Lexington Avenue and Twenty-Sixth Street, on the East Side of Manhattan, was the headquarters of the New York National Guard First Battalion, Sixty-Ninth Infantry Regiment. The families and friends of those who worked at the World Trade Center and had yet to return home came to the armory to file missing-persons reports. The hope was to match a name to the face of a very small number of the wounded being treated at city hospitals, those without any clear identification. The building was designated as a family assistance center, and it drew everyone still holding out hope.

The families arrived early. They refused to be mourners, not yet. In lines snaking around the entire block, they carried evidence of their love, and proofs of identity. There were pictures and letters, medical records and physical descriptions. Hundreds carried flyers advertising their missing, lives whittled down to the physical facts of being: name, age, height, weight, topped by a single picture. Nearly all the flyers ended with a list of phone numbers to call.

The notices were placed everywhere: on telephone poles and mailboxes, on street lamps and tree trunks. They formed a pleading and dense collage on the walls of the armory itself.

Jeff came to join the somber line of those waiting to file reports and submit to police interviews. Years later, he'd recall nearby residents who came out of their apartment buildings with sandwiches and cookies to offer, a way to try to comfort those touched most by the assault on their city. The memory would bring tears to his eyes.

After speaking with two NYPD detectives and providing all the information he could, he left the armory. To the south, smoke from the pile stained the sky. In inaccessible pockets far below the ground, the fires would burn for months to come.

Thursday morning. Two days. Nearly fifty hours.

At 10:45 a.m., the doorbell rang. Jeff was in the city, covering the terrain as best he could. Welles's mother was home, exhausted with worry, when she heard it.

Alison walked to the door and saw Harry Wanamaker standing outside, covered in silt, ash soaked into the fiber of his gear and caked on his turnouts. Wanamaker stood with his helmet under his arm, his eyes straight upon her. He'd come directly from the scorched ground of the Trade Center complex. The only stop he'd made before coming to the house on Birchwood was at his own, to take off his boots and put on clean socks. He didn't want to track dirt across her floor.

Less than three months before, on a June night, he'd stood on the deck of his fireboat surrounded by his friends from Empire Hook and Ladder. He had toured them around Lower Manhattan, and stood next to Welles, arm to arm, with the Twin Towers behind them, soaring and dark. He was relaxed, the collar of his blue shirt open, a smile creasing his face, Welles's own grin wide beside him.

Now Harry stood outside the door looking at Welles's mother, his face drawn and exhausted. Her breath caught at the sight of him. She opened the door and ushered him in.

"Harry," she said. "My God . . . what are you doing here?"

"I've just come back," he said.

"Let me get you in here, and get you some food."

He walked inside. "I just want to tell you . . . we're doing everything we can."

They sat and talked for an hour, Harry trying to eat the lunch she quickly made for him. He tried to explain the collapse of the buildings, the unthinkable scope of the ruins, the way the fireboat rushed to the scene upon receiving the first call. But over and over, Harry said the same words in a fragment or a sentence, a pledge and a wish. He gave them voice to make them real. He said it, so together they might believe it.

"We're going to find him."

The winds blew gently through the Hudson Valley, rippling the waters, stirring the trees. The final Saturday in September was cool, the promise of autumn deepening, as the people gathered, carrying their emptiness inside.

Light poured through the stained-glass window, rounded and majestic, filling the sanctuary with soft beams from above the arched wooden doors.

Grace Episcopal Church in Nyack, a century and a half old, stood in its place on First Avenue, its massive stone façade stern and comforting. It was the Crowther family's church even before moving to town, a place of worship and fellowship, of community and solidarity.

On this day, September 29, 2001, it was a place to say good-bye. More than a thousand came, filling the sanctuary's space, with more waiting outside in brilliant sunshine. The church drew them together as the central point in so many circles of Welles's life.

They arrived to pay tribute, and to mourn.

The Reverend Richard Gressle, the church's rector, spoke.

"Welles, who befriended the world, has taken that step beyond," he said. "It is our responsibility that we honor who he was by befriending one another and the world."

Welles's sister Honor, two years younger, delivered the eulogy. She stood at the front of the church, looking out at her parents and sister, her aunts and uncles, and the rows of pews behind them, filled and silent, save for the sobbing and the echo of her own voice.

She spoke with heart and humor, describing not a saint but a brother. On September 11, driving with her boyfriend, Rick, from their apartment in Mount Kisco to her parents' house, she was filled with a terrible sense of certainty. She knew, even before reaching Nyack, that her brother was gone. She would fight to keep hope, but as they crossed the Hudson, his voice came to her, Welles speaking to her. She felt him. The message was clear. She should be the one to speak for him. Whenever the moment came, it should be her. And she made another decision on that drive. Honor knew that she would one day name her first child after her brother. As soon as she arrived home, she began composing lines in her mind, many she would say now. She recalled the bright times and the sibling fights, the lacrosse practices and the training runs. They were part of daily life, and they would live on in memory.

"He helped me understand our bumps and bruises were badges of courage," she said, looking out at the assembly in its black and muted dress.

"His ability to laugh led him to see the best in any situation. . . . He could brighten a room from the house next door."

After she finished, others followed. Friends of Welles's laughed and wept, their numbness thawing if only for an hour or two, opening themselves to receive his absence now as something final. Near the end of the memorial service, Jeff watched as Bill Cassidy, chaplain for the Empire Hook and Ladder's company and for the entire Nyack Fire Department as well, walked to the front of the church. Jeff had been the company chaplain once too, and had stood where Cassidy was now. He had delivered the words he was now about to hear, in tribute to other fallen firefighters. All those services had been for men much older. None had been for his son.

Cassidy recited an order of the service Jeff had shared many times before.

> The last alarm has sounded for our brother.
> To Welles has come that last call.
> It is the call from which there is no turning away,
> The imperative and final order,
> Of the great chief and captain of us all . . .

The words rang through the church.

Welles's uncle Bosley gave the final reading, straining with emotion, delivering lines from Tennyson's elegy "Crossing the Bar."

The remarks done, the echoes quieted, mourners stood and turned to leave. Alison walked from the pew and saw the doors open, flooding the entire space with a dazzling light. The world beyond the church's threshold was difficult to glimpse, its reality blank and flat. But as she got closer to the exit, she began to discern figures standing along the sidewalk, lining the entire frontage of the church lot. There was a color guard and an honor guard, and there were firefighters as far as she could see, standing in uniform dress. They stood still and solemn, flanking the ladder truck from Empire Hook and Ladder No. 1.

The sight overwhelmed her and her body buckled before Jeff caught her. She beheld the large American flag flying from the truck, rolling with the breezes off the river. It was placed prominently, proudly.

There was no casket over which to drape it.

SEVEN

HALF A YEAR had passed. On Sunday, March 17, Alison had been watching the news at home, her hunger for information never sated. By this time, much of the compacted debris of the pile at ground zero had been cleared. A last major area remained, near an access road built within the acreage of the gaping hole. For those who worked at the pile, and for the victims' families especially, it was an anxious time, a fear deepening that they would never receive their loved ones' remains. Much of the pile was gone.

The news report stated that excavation would begin in the area underneath the central ramp leading down into the pit. Without knowing the exact geography, Alison was still struck by the report. She sensed that maybe this was the place where Welles would be. She'd learned not to hold back from such feelings. To keep them inside would be to collapse from their weight. Whatever she felt, she acknowledged and accepted. She gave the feelings voice, most often to her husband.

She looked at him after hearing the report and without hesitation made a declaration she'd never made before.

"Jeff," she said. "They're going to find Welles. This week. They're going to find him."

He looked at her, hearing her certainty, even if he didn't share the same expectation. Of course he wanted his son back, in the most desperate way. But he didn't make these declarations the way she did.

"Well, okay," he said, accepting her belief.

On Friday of that same week, March 22, Alison was accompanying her youngest daughter, Paige, on a visit to the State University of New York in nearby Purchase. SUNY Purchase was a magnet for aspiring artists, with one of the strongest performing arts programs in the country. Paige, an elite dancer considering a life in professional ballet, was auditioning for the university's dance conservatory.

Alison was reading, waiting, when Paige joined her during a break. A few minutes later, her cell phone rang. It was the Crowthers' housekeeper calling.

"There's a policeman here, at the door," she said.

Alison wondered if one of the family's dogs had gotten loose and was marauding through the neighborhood.

The policeman came on the line. "Mrs. Crowther," he said. In the tone of those two words, she knew it was something else entirely. She stepped away from Paige, the phone to her ear.

"Mrs. Crowther," the voice said, "your son's body has been recovered at ground zero."

She fought desperately not to cry. Trying to collect herself, she thought of Paige and her audition, not wanting to cast any shadow over her daughter, who'd suffered in her own way through these long months. She didn't want to take an ounce of light from her daughter's day, but how not to? She brought herself back to the phone in her hand and found courage enough to ask the question. "How did they identify him?"

"By his fingerprints."

"His fingerprints? Oh my God . . ." It was certain. It was her son.

The call ended. She stood there, overwhelmed, but determined to be present for Paige. To support her daughter in her moment as best she could.

Later in the day, Paige sensed that something had happened, and she asked her mother what was wrong. Alison could hold it in no longer. She looked at her daughter.

"They found Welles," she said.

The Crowthers' first child was born on a Tuesday. He died on a Tuesday. On a Tuesday, his body was first found, on the nineteenth, his number in all things since boyhood, chosen for nearly every jersey he wore, even down to the apartment number he shared with Chuck Platz in the city.

The Crowthers had a hard trip to the city's chief medical examiner's office on East Twenty-Sixth Street. It was the place where death was made official, and where its cause, manner, and mechanism were determined for the entire jurisdiction of New York City.

They came to the Manhattan office to find out as much as they could about their son's end, or at least as much as they could bear. How many details could they endure, how many facts could they accept, beyond the final one?

Together, they passed into the offices, with its motto written on the lobby wall: "Science Serving Justice."

They met with a medical examiner.

Where was he found?

The body was recovered in the debris of what had been the lobby of the South Tower.

For them, this answer was a revelation.

The lobby. Could that really be? From 104 floors above, when the second plane struck, all the way down to the ground?

Somehow, he had made it down.

How close was he to getting out? To surviving? Could he

have made it? Why didn't he? What stopped him? What was he doing? Who was he with?

Jeff felt the answer immediately, even as so many other questions flooded through his mind: He was helping.

They learned more. Welles's body was found that March in an area of the pit where firefighters' remains were recovered. Most specifically, he lay close to FDNY assistant chief Donald Burns. Burns, sixty-one, one of the most respected members of the entire department, had been a responding commander during the 1993 attack at the World Trade Center in the North Tower, decorated many times over in his thirty-nine years serving. As a citywide commander, he covered all major incidents and emergencies across the five boroughs. As the chief in charge of the South Tower on September 11, he had set up a command post in the tower lobby, helping to lead the evacuation effort for thousands who survived, as well as to guide the department's responding personnel through the challenge of fighting a raging fire nearly a quarter mile up in the sky. Burns's body was discovered in an area of rubble beside the remains of ten other firefighters. And those of Welles Crowther.

John Ryan, the commander of the Port Authority Police Department's rescue and recovery operation at ground zero, who covered the pile from that September day all the way through the following spring, knew every inch of the tower lobby down to the tile. He was familiar with the area where

*Firefighters combing through the rubble of the
World Trade Center on September 14, 2001.*

the command post had been set up that morning, and the debris field where Burns, Welles, and others were recovered.

"The command post location was selected," Ryan said, "so that responders coming in from the street would be able to go to it with relative ease."

He understood what that meant for the families of those recovered in or near that spot: they were close to making it out of the building, to the safety of the street, to the rest of their lives.

He estimated the distance to the exits at seventy-five feet. "People found in that area," Ryan said, "were seconds away from being clear."

To be so close to an escape but to remain inside was not coincidence. Likely, it was a choice. Welles made it. He was helping.

He was at work.

On a gray March day, there would be another service for Welles at Grace Episcopal Church in Nyack, where his ashes would later be immured.

Welles's parents were there, beside Honor and her boyfriend, Rick, the man she would later marry. Paige was there too, with Amy Rappaport, a lifelong friend. Welles's remains were wrapped in an American flag, resting in a plain wooden box, humbler, lesser than a coffin. It's a moment, and a sight, Paige has never forgotten.

"I remember thinking to myself," she said, "*my big brother fits in that small box*. The box was too small for him. . . ." She paused, crying at the memory. "It was not substantial enough for my big brother and his big personality and his big size. It just seemed like a box that a four-foot child could fit in. . . ."

The Reverend Richard Gressle, who had presided over the memorial service at Grace Episcopal Church back in the fall, joined the family, along with the funeral director and staff. They were there to receive Welles, pray over him, and send him onward. Not the thousand mourners who'd gathered back in September, not the public farewell. He lay now in the close grip of family.

On Sunday morning of Memorial Day weekend, 2002, *The New York Times* landed on the Crowthers' doorstep, as it always did.

There was an understanding in the Crowther house that Jeff read the paper first. He liked to go through the Sunday *Times* in a certain order.

In the months since September, newspaper stories about the terrorist attacks remained a staple, but they came with less frequency now. The city was trying to find its way through recovery, even as the hole in Lower Manhattan remained. Alison was still gripped by every story, but Jeff had a different reaction. For the most part, he turned the page, the reminder painful and un-welcome. The sadness was challenge enough without the news adding to it.

Jeff opened the paper that morning and saw a feature piece on the front page with the large headline "Fighting to Live as the Towers Died."

The story, written by *Times* reporters Jim Dwyer, Eric Lipton, Kevin Flynn, James Glanz, and Ford Fessenden, was several thousand words long. It would become the basis for the seminal book *102 Minutes*, written by Dwyer and Flynn, a comprehensive and masterful chronicle of reporting and writing documenting the space of time between the first plane strike and the second tower's collapse, filled with direct accounts from survivors as well as dispatches from the families, colleagues, and friends of those lost. The book would become the definitive account of the fight for survival as the buildings burned and then fell.

As much respect as Jeff had for the *Times*, he knew right away that he wouldn't read the piece. By this point, more than eight months after Welles's death, his reaction was nearly reflexive. He also knew that Alison would want to scan every word.

"Alison," he called to her, "there's an article in the paper here. You may want to see this."

She saw the headline, took the front section of the paper, and went to their bedroom. Atop the bed, she sat up and began reading through the minute-by-minute account of what was happening in the towers as the attacks unfolded. For all the information she'd digested already, all the reports she'd consumed in print and on air, she'd never read anything like this. The detail was breathtaking, heartbreaking. The piece placed her inside the buildings, side by side with survivors and victims.

She began to read the accounts of those on the 78th floor of the South Tower, the sky lobby, where Flight 175's lower wing exploded into the building, slashing through the crowd waiting for the elevators. She read of the obliterating intensity of the impact, but also of several who somehow survived the plane's strike. She stopped reading for a moment, going back to the phone message Welles left her. The time. With the chronology provided so clearly in the article, laid out for her more plainly than she'd ever seen before, she reconsidered the timing of Welles's day.

He'd left the message for her after the plane hit the South Tower. She knew that his remains had been found in the ruins of the ground-floor lobby. She began to imagine his path down from the 104th floor on the stairs, and likely his coming upon the distress and terror of the sky lobby. She believed that if he saw any of the devastation depicted so vividly in the article, there would be no way for him to pass by. He'd respond. That was his training. That was her son.

And that's when she read it. Two-thirds of the way through the long piece, in the 128th paragraph of the story. She stopped, staring at the two sentences:

> A mysterious man appeared at one point, his mouth and nose covered with a red handkerchief. He was looking for a fire extinguisher.

A red handkerchief.

Jeff was in the kitchen when he heard the shout.

"Jeff! Jeff! Get in here!"

He came rushing to the bedroom, where Alison had the paper open in front of her.

"I found Welles," she said. She read aloud the portion of the article, and pointed to the description of the mysterious man in the ruins and fires of the 78th-floor sky lobby, his face covered with the red cloth.

Jeff tried to be measured in the face of her excitement.

"That has to be Welles," she said. "That's where he would've been, the 78th floor, that sky lobby. With the bandanna."

"No," he replied, as evenly as he could. "We don't know that. We don't know that's him. It could've been anyone else there."

"Maybe," she acknowledged. "I know we don't know if it's him. But I know. I know it's him."

Thanks to the *Times*'s reporting, she also knew the names of two survivors who mentioned seeing the mysterious man and his red handkerchief, a man they saw trying to lead others to safety. The survivors were among the eighteen in or above the plane's impact zone who miraculously made it out. Their names were Ling Young and Judy Wein.

Alison was going to find them.

Alison focused initially on Judy Wein because there was no clear lead for Ling Young in the *Times* article. Judy was listed in the piece as working for Aon Corporation, on the 103rd floor of the South Tower. She called Aon first.

"Judy isn't here," came the reply.

Alison tried to explain the nature of her inquiry, but how? The company had lost scores of its employees in the attacks, every victim with a family who wanted to know about those final hours, about where he was, how she fought, what they felt. How could she press into that wound for her own answers?

She mentioned what she'd read in the *Times* and asked if there was any way the office might pass on her contact information. She told the receptionist she might know who helped to save Judy Wein, and she needed to talk to her. The receptionist took down her information and the call ended.

Later that day, Judy called back. While Judy had spoken to

the *Times*'s Eric Lipton, giving her account of survival directly to the reporter, the interview was in fact a rarity. Despite the onslaught of media requests and inquiries that came asking her to share her story, Judy rarely granted interviews.

In the aftermath of her escape, she'd shared every detail with her husband, Gerry Sussman, from her hospital bed. From then on, Gerry became an integral part of telling her story. Gerry handled nearly all the requests, and when Judy agreed to cooperate, primarily it was Gerry who served as the intermediary.

According to Gerry, Judy had a deep, personal motivation for giving the *Times* interview directly.

"She was hoping that they would uncover the man with the red handkerchief."

Judy listened as Alison described some of the simplest facts about Welles. She was trying not to overload Judy or pressure her into any kind of confirmation. She could hear Jeff's voice in her head, urging caution and the proper dose of uncertainty. She told herself she was prepared to hear what she hoped not to: that it wasn't him. But she needed to know.

As Judy remembered, the man was white, young, fit, as best she could tell. Alison felt herself getting closer to the answer.

"I think it may have been my son who saved you," she said on the phone. "He was always carrying a red bandanna with him, even in his business suit. He was a trained firefighter. From what I read, I just . . . I believe it was him."

The red bandanna was fixed in Judy's mind and vision. She wanted to know the man's identity too, of course, to know who had emerged from the smoke to lead her to safety. Though if this was the man, the identification would also carry a sad truth.

She could never thank him.

On the call, Judy told Alison there was an e-mail chain connecting a group of South Tower survivors, the few who'd made it out from the 78th-floor sky lobby or above. She and Gerry would send the inquiry down the line, to see who might have seen the man, if anyone else spotted a red bandanna. Then Alison asked:

"Can I send you a picture of my son?"

She got the address, looked for a recent photo, and mailed it out.

Judy Wein looked at the photo that spilled from the envelope, a picture of Welles from his Boston College graduation, taken in the spring of 1999, a little more than two years before September 11. He was smiling, proud, facing into the future.

Gerry recalled his wife's reaction, and her response. "Although it was dark and smoky and hard to see very clearly in the sky lobby," Gerry said, "Judy did get a clear picture of Welles after he brought her into the well-lit stairwell." He wasn't cov-

Welles with his mother, Alison, at his college graduation.

ering his face with the red handkerchief then. She remembered what he looked like.

"And she identified him," Gerry said. His wife was clear, without doubt, certain. She knew.

"Yes," she told her husband, "that was the man." Gerry paused a moment in his recollection.

"It was very sad," he said. "Until that time we really didn't know if he'd survived."

To be certain, Judy and Gerry sent the photo of Welles out through the survivors' group e-mail chain. Was there anyone else who escaped the building who remembered seeing this man in the picture and could identify him as the one who led the way out of the sky lobby, into Stairway A, and down?

Judy knew two others, Gigi Singer and Ed Nicholls, both injured in the impact, who had been close behind her as she'd made her way to the stairwell and began the descent. She didn't know who else had been guided to the stairs by the man with the red bandanna. She knew Singer and Nicholls might not have seen the man, but both followed her after she heard the man's instructions. Likely, none of them would've found the way without his guiding them. That's what she told her husband.

"The people who went down with Judy," he said, "were actually saved by Welles, although they may not realize that. I don't know how they actually got into the stairwell, but certainly Judy was the first one in and then these people followed, and they went down the stairs with Judy."

After the photo went out, a reply came quickly, not from a survivor but from one of her children. Richard Young, Ling Young's son, saw the e-mail and wondered if this was the man his mother had told him about from the beginning, the man who walked with her down the stairs.

Since making it down, Ling had been consumed by the struggle to recover.

"I was not just burned," Ling said. "They were thermal burns, which means . . . I was cooked." She looked down at the scars on her arm. "I had a lot of complications, lot of infections."

Richard asked his mother the question: "Doesn't this sound like the man who took you down?"

It did, but she wasn't sure. Judy's story was different from hers. Judy stressed the sight of the handkerchief, the red bandanna, across the rescuer's face. It was the most significant image of her rescuer, at least as Ling read it. Ling had seen the man's face too, plainly, in the clear air of the stairwell when they reached the 61st floor. She looked directly at him before he left for the climb back up. That's what she remembered. She thought he might've had a red bandanna, but it wasn't covering his face as they descended the stairs, as he encouraged her to keep going, not to separate from him. She believed he might have had a handkerchief pulled down below his chin, wrapped around his neck, but she wasn't sure. She needed to see his face again to be certain.

Richard showed his mother the attached photo in the message.

Both understood how crucial the answer was. To say yes without absolute certainty would be wrong for all involved. They wanted to help a grieving mother desperate to understand her son's final hour, but they needed to be sure.

Ling couldn't say with certitude. The graduation photo was somehow too formal, the young man in cap and gown too put together, too well groomed. In the escape from the lobby's flames and devastation, the man she remembered reflected the chaos—his short hair matted with sweat, his face flushed. He'd stripped down to his T-shirt. She needed to get a different look at the man to compare with the image trapped in her head.

At Ling's behest, Richard called Alison. He explained he was reaching out, due to his mother's condition, trying to gain more clarity, to confirm whether the man who led Ling down the stairs was in fact Welles. Richard and Ling were determined to confirm Alison's hope, but only if it was true.

"'My mother thinks this may be the man,'" Alison recalled Richard saying. "'But can you send another photograph?'"

Ling wanted a different image, she told her son, "a casual picture of him, something that's not all dressed up, like in a suit and tie." Alison thought she knew the right shot. "I'll overnight it to you." The first image that came to mind was Welles from a year before, standing beside Harry Wanamaker, Jr., on the deck of Marine 1's *John D. McKean*, on their cruise around Lower Manhattan. Behind them, the dark towers of the World Trade Center loomed, soaring into the darkness.

She made a copy of the photo, but altered it first. Alison didn't want the full picture to add in any way to Ling's pain, or influence her decision. She enlarged it from the center until the towers were cropped from the frame.

Then she sent it to Richard and Ling.

After receiving the second photo, Richard prepared to show it to his mother. He understood the stakes of her reaction, for Ling and for Alison. During their phone conversation, Alison had stressed to Richard that she didn't want to place any pressure on Ling. She was ready to accept a different answer. She could live with no.

Richard had his back to Ling, holding the picture, and then turned quickly around. He wanted to see his mother's immediate, raw reaction. Ling looked at the image of Welles's face aboard the boat, the smile broad and easy, the early summer evening.

Ling looked at the man she'd never seen before September 11, whom she'd last seen turning around to go back up the stairs to the blood and fire. The face. She looked at nothing more than the face.

One word: *Yes*.

"I looked at it very carefully," Ling said, recalling the moment.

"My son says, 'Are you sure? Are you one hundred percent sure? You know, you can't be wrong.'"

She didn't hesitate. She was certain.

"If you're going to ask me ten times? Yes. One hundred times? Yes. Because that's the face. . . . That was him, there was no question in my mind."

She didn't know how long it was until the next thought entered her mind, but it would stay there for years to come.

He saved my life.

Before calling Alison, Ling reached out to Judy first, to share what she saw in the photo, and to build a time line. They could help each other piece together the sequence that led them out of the inferno of the sky lobby, into Stairway A, down to clear air and beyond, to the ground floor, and into the ambulance they shared.

Judy's story shone a light on Ling's own path down the stairwell. Talking with each other, they were struck anew by the improbability of their escape. Ling was the first to answer Welles's call in the lobby, following him as he led the way into the stairwell, walking with her and the other tall, thin man she didn't know. He walked with them, carrying the woman on his back, until they reached the 61st floor. Then he told her he was going back up. He left to make the ascent back up seventeen floors to 78, to see whom else he could help.

When he emerged through the smoke and fire a second time, it was Judy who heard him call out, a man with a red bandanna covering his face against the smoke. She heard his instruction, urgent but strong and clear. They were among the first words she told her husband from her hospital bed hours after the buildings collapsed.

"She heard him call out to everyone," Gerry said. "And he said, 'Everyone who can stand, stand now. If you can help others, do so.' Those were his exact words as she told them to me that afternoon."

At least two others followed Judy into the stairwell, by her account guided there by Welles. Later, after reaching the clear air below the 61st floor, she saw a fire extinguisher. She remembered thinking how strange it was to see it, there in the stairwell.

Ling told Judy that this was the fire extinguisher Welles asked her to carry, the one that proved too heavy to lug down. The fire extinguisher helped them understand the sequence—it was Ling who'd gone down first, and then Judy. Welles had helped two different groups of survivors find the stairwell. When Judy reached the 50th floor, she encountered firefighters who were on their way up, exhausted from the climb and the heavy gear they carried. These were the firefighters who told her and the others to continue down to the 40th floor, where they'd find a working service elevator.

More questions remained. How many others had Welles helped? How many of the survivors from the sky lobby had followed them after Welles's original instruction? They couldn't know.

Ling's son Richard made the call to Alison.

He had a few final questions for her, to be thorough, before sharing his mother's answer. Alison breathed deeply, trying to slow down, to root herself in the moment, not to race ahead.

"This red handkerchief that's been mentioned in the article," Richard said to her. "Was it solid red?"

"No," Alison said immediately. "If it was solid red, then that's not Welles. It would have been a bandanna pattern . . ."

"Okay," Richard said. Then another question.

"He was wearing a T-shirt. What kind of T-shirt would it be?"

She knew instantly. He'd worn the same style his whole life, it seemed.

"He would have been wearing a crewneck, short-sleeve Brooks Brothers–type white T-shirt." She added, "Not V-neck or tank top." Richard said that matched his mother's description.

No more questions. Just the answer.

"My mother says it's him," Richard told her. "She says this is the man."

❧ ✦ ✦ ❧

Nine and a half months after Judy and Ling shared their cramped, frightened ride in the back of the ambulance, rushing away from the perimeter of the Trade Center complex toward the hospital, they were meeting again in person. Others would join them too—their families and their hosts. On June

23, 2002, they were spending a warm, sunny Sunday afternoon in Upper Nyack, guests of the Crowther family.

Alison had seen Ling and her family already. After their phone conversation, she asked if she could visit with them. She wanted to share so much about Welles, about his life before that moment when he and Ling met. She wanted them to understand her son, as best a mother could explain her child, wondering too if she was being selfish in her need to share him, but Richard's reaction dismissed that concern, according to Alison.

"Richard said to me, 'My mom wanted to know who this man was for a long time.'" The entire family wanted to know.

Alison took some family photo albums to share the different stages of Welles's life—the boy with his fire truck under the Christmas tree, the one wearing the bandanna across his forehead, the budding lacrosse player, the college kid, the young professional. For Alison, they were portraits of wonder for new eyes to see.

She traveled down to New York Hospital, Cornell Burn Center, where Ling was preparing for her seventh skin-graft surgery, to meet Ling, Richard, and their family for lunch. The two women sat beside each other, face-to-face for the first time since Ling made the identification. Alison looked at Ling in awe. She had faced the same fire, breathed the same air, and walked the same steps as her son, and she'd made it down. She said the first thing that came to her mind.

"Thank you so much," Alison said. "I just want to . . ." Her voice trailed away for a few seconds. "I'm so happy to meet you and . . . thank you. Thank you for taking the time to meet with me." She remembered what she carried with her. "I just brought these albums to show you . . . to show you my Welles."

He was almost the sole subject of that first meeting. Ling said virtually nothing about the scene in the sky lobby then, about what she'd endured, about the attacks and the suffering they'd brought her. Alison spoke about Welles, and Ling and her family listened, expressing their gratitude to her as best they could. For raising him. For his help. For his choice.

Now, a few weeks later, they were together again in a larger group—these three families sitting on the shaded patio behind the house on Birchwood, sharing lunch. Ling in a wheelchair with her husband, Don, and their children; Judy with her husband, Gerry; and Alison, Jeff, Honor, Paige, and a few others, all sharing the same table.

At that table, the others listened as Judy and Ling began to talk about the horrors they each endured that day.

Both said Welles had been the only commanding voice they heard, the only one anywhere on the floor who seemed to understand what to do and where to go. With their families around them, each told Alison and Jeff, over and over again, what Welles had done, what he meant to them, what they owed him.

When lunch was over, the tears dried and the plates cleared, they decided there was one more place to go. Judy and Gerry went with Alison, and Ling and her family with Jeff, and the group left the house and headed on a short drive to First Avenue in Nyack. They pulled up outside the stone façade of Grace Episcopal Church. Together, they walked inside, the sanctuary warmer but filled with nearly the same slant of light it had held nine months before during the service. The group came to a spot and turned its gaze upon the church's memorial wall. Jeff and Alison pointed to the place where Welles's ashes lay inside.

The Crowthers were so grateful for the light that had been cast on Welles's final hours. To be able to look into the faces of these two lives he saved, to know their names, to hear their voices. But there were still so many unanswered questions. How many others on the 78th floor might never have seen the red bandanna but had heard a voice, or seen a hand, or followed a lead that came from Welles?

There were clues. Two other survivors followed Judy to the stairwell, at least. One of them was Ed Nicholls. He had been in the sky lobby waiting for an elevator when the plane's impact blasted him off his feet. He had a distinct memory of a man's voice directing him and the others to the stairwell, but not a clear recollection of what he looked like.

Even without more answers, there was a story, and Jeff and Alison wanted to share it—for its message, to help them heal and to help others heal too. They had been granted something so few others had: an understanding of their son's final actions, and their consequences. There was great pride in that knowledge, and no small degree of comfort. They believed the story might prove a point even beyond their son's sacrifice. So many responded by running toward the threat and into the peril. This was the story of one responder, not assigned or asked, not dispatched from a station house or dressed in gear, who did the same and never returned. Alison believed she knew who would be interested in telling it.

Back in March, she'd met Jane Lerner, a veteran reporter with the *Journal News*, a newspaper based in the Lower Hudson Valley and part of the USA Today Network across the country. Jane was assigned to cover the small ceremony at Grace Episcopal after Welles's body was recovered and cremated. Her story, "Volunteer Firefighter Found at Ground Zero Laid to Rest," ran in the Sunday edition of the paper, quoting Alison and rendering the scene with skill and compassion. The piece made an impression on the family. In June, Alison shared with Jane the story about her son, the mysterious man noted in *The New York Times* who'd helped to save others on the 78th floor before losing his life in the South Tower's collapse. Alison told her about Welles, about the red handkerchief he carried since he was a little boy, and, after the planes hit, how he'd swapped his role from equities trader to volunteer firefighter, using the bandanna to cover his face from the smoke and dust as he led others to safety.

The 1,565-word piece ran under the headline "Bandanna Links Acts of Courage," and traced Welles's actions up until, and through, September 11. With quotes from Ling Young and Judy Wein, the story identified Welles for the first time publicly as the man who'd saved their lives, and those of an unknown number of others.

"He saved so many people," Ling was quoted in the article as saying, "but he didn't save himself.

"His whole life was ahead. It's such a tragedy."

The story was now told. Soon, it would spread.

EIGHT

TEN MONTHS AND one day after the towers fell, on July 12, 2002, many of Welles's childhood and high school friends from Nyack gathered inside the chapel as one of them stood at the altar, awaiting his bride's approach.

Rob Lewis was getting married. He'd known Welles nearly all his life in Nyack, all the way back to playing T-ball games together and being in the same Cub Scout troop, where Alison had served as den mother. As each grew, their bond strengthened over afternoons of pond hockey and through the seasons of their lacrosse careers. After graduation they moved in separate directions, but stayed in touch, part of the larger Nyack crew who saw one another during holidays and summers and reunions back home.

When the planes struck the towers, Rob was forty-six hundred miles east, stationed as a soldier in Kosovo. He remembered a group of fifty soldiers packed into a room in their camp, watching the smoke and fire unfurl across the television screen. He'd never felt so maddeningly far from his country.

Just a few weeks before Rob's wedding, the story of Welles's final hour began to make the rounds from one friend to another. What he'd done. Whom he'd saved. The story was at once astonishing and real. The friends and their families had to share it with one another, and with others outside the circle too, with people who never knew Welles.

When the bride and groom were introduced at the reception, Rob walked in beaming, his arms raised high. In his hand, he held a red bandanna. All the groomsmen, including his brother, Steven, and his army buddy Jimmy Silliman, and all the Nyack gang—Karim Raoul, Jody Steinglass, Willie Hopkins, Matt Dickey, Michael Barch, Matt Drowne—had red bandannas in their jacket pockets. They lifted them high.

They were carrying Welles to the party.

And so it started.

The story pushed past the friends, beyond Boston and Nyack and Rockland County, down the Lower Hudson Valley into New York City, and from there, across the country. CNN.

USA Today. ABC News. There was a flurry of coverage in particular as the first anniversary of the attack arrived, spotlighting the tale of a young man who'd climbed back up as others went down. Together with the help of friends and a close board of advisers, Jeff and Alison created a charitable trust in Welles's name, determined to find and build good from his death, to share the meaning of his life and his sacrifice. Their goal was not just to remember but, through memory, to give. Starting the year after his death, the trust began granting scholarships to Nyack students who embodied Welles's values and passions, and making gifts and grants to other nonprofits sharing his example. The work it took to create the trust provided its own measure of healing.

For those Welles had left behind, the bandanna mattered; its knot tied together his memory and example to those who still held them, and might perpetuate them. His friends began carrying his story inside the handkerchief's folds.

John Scott, his teammate in Nyack, ran a youth hockey program in Raleigh, North Carolina, and told every player about the bandanna and the man behind it. He did the same for the women's college softball team he helped at his alma mater, Barton College, in Wilson, North Carolina. "For every team I coach, nobody wears number nineteen," he said, "and I tell the kids why."

Tyler Jewell, his friend and teammate at BC, represented the United States as a snowboarder in the Winter Olympics in Turin in 2006, competing in the men's parallel giant slalom. Jewell wore a red bandanna around his neck for the world to see as he slashed down the mountain.

Matt O'Keefe, a college classmate and avid golfer, tied a bandanna around the handle of his golf bag the week Welles's body was recovered, and never removed it. After BC, he founded an apparel company for CrossFit athletes, several of whom would wear the bandanna design O'Keefe created. "They have such an attachment to that story," O'Keefe said. "It's become a symbol of strength and courage."

Chris Varmon, another hockey teammate in Nyack, helped to create the Red Bandanna Skate for young and old players of all skill levels in Rockland County, an event to celebrate sportsmanship, team spirit, and passion for the game. Each year, most of the skaters wear bandannas beneath their helmets, as Welles often did.

Matt Drowne had a tattoo of the bandanna inked between his shoulders, with Welles's initials placed at the bottom. As a teacher and administrator working with special needs students, he began a red bandanna award, given each year to a child demonstrating exceptional courage.

Jessica Alberti, a friend from BC, remembered Welles as a kind voice during the challenges of their college years. After learning what Welles had done, she pushed herself to run her first marathon. In 2002, she crossed the line in Central Park after 26.2 miles through New York City, with Welles's name written across her shirt and a small red bandanna attached. "I felt like if he could do something that amazing," Jessica said, "I should be able to do this." In 2004, she and others helped to start the annual Red Bandanna 5k at Boston College, now one of the biggest events on campus each fall.

Tim Epstein, a friend who lived in the same freshman dorm at BC, would present Welles's story to the board of the Fetzer Institute, a foundation working to promote love and forgiveness around the world. The presentation led Fetzer to help fund a character-based curriculum that teaches lessons of service and compassion through Welles's story and the bandanna symbol to schools around the country. When Tim's wife gave birth to their daughter, he called Jeff and Alison from the hospital to ask a favor. "I wanted to make sure that they would be comfortable with us naming her Madeline Welles," he said. "They gave the blessing, and we announced her to the world thereafter." Before 2012, there were no more than five children in the United States who were given the name Welles in a single year. Between 2012 and 2014, there were thirty-five newborns given the name—many from families who'd never met Welles or the Crowthers.

Chris Reynolds knew Welles from childhood but understood the symbol of the bandanna differently from anyone else.

A friend growing up, a teammate in football and hockey, he remembered joking in a high school locker room that he and the other guys "would be flipping burgers, and Welles will be making a difference in the world someday." The others laughed, Welles maybe the loudest. But Chris would make his own considerable mark. He too became a volunteer firefighter as a teenager, and knew immediately it would be his career. After attending college, getting the FDNY application, taking the exams, staying in shape, waiting, the call came. His first posting was with New York City EMS, which had just come under the FDNY's control. A short time later, in February 2001, he made the move to "probie school," the department's probationary firefighter program. After ten weeks he graduated, and in the spring he received his first appointment. Engine 80, Harlem. A lifelong dream achieved, was how he described it.

The morning of September 11, Chris was at work when a second alarm transmitted, indicating a plane had struck the World Trade Center. He and others turned to the house television.

"We see the smoke coming out of the building," he remembered, "and everything that's happening downtown, and we start getting ready. We're going to get a response to head down to the Trade Center. We did a refill on all of the medical equipment and getting ready to go, waiting for the dispatcher to send us downtown.

"And then we saw the second plane hit."

As one of the last units left in Upper Manhattan, Chris's company endured an agonizing wait before being dispatched to the scene. He arrived with his company Tuesday night, and didn't leave for five days.

He wasn't there when Welles's body was found, but he knew the area well and understood where Welles was, and why.

"I know he was found with Ladder 4 in the lobby," he said. "I'm sure he was standing right there with his brothers, waiting to go back up and help. . . . I'm sure he was helping the chief, the command post, and the officers of the companies and the firemen, to let them know what the best route was, because he came down from the upper floors."

Reynolds paused.

"He had every opportunity to leave and he didn't. He stayed and he put others first, and that's something you either have or you don't. He had it, and he used it."

NINE

ON A DECEMBER day in 2006, Jeff and Alison led a small caravan traveling south to the city for a ceremony they never thought they'd witness. They gathered at MetroTech Plaza in downtown Brooklyn, off Flatbush Avenue, ten days before Christmas for an event held just once before in the 141 years since the department's founding. It was only the second time the FDNY would posthumously name someone an honorary member of its ranks.

The idea had its seed in a chance encounter. Lee Ielpi, who'd joined the FDNY in 1970, had lost his son Jonathan in the attacks when he responded as a member of FDNY Squad 288.

Months later, Jeff went downtown to the Family Room, on

Liberty Plaza, a space adjacent to ground zero where victims' loved ones could come for privacy and reflection. One of the rooms was solely for immediate family, its walls covered with photos and mementos. Jeff brought a photo in a simple wooden frame to add to the collection. While there, Jeff encountered Lee Ielpi, and the two began to talk. Lee explained that he too had lost his son in the attacks, among the 343 FDNY members who were killed. Jeff told him that Welles was a volunteer firefighter, and that his remains were found on March 19 in the lobby's rubble.

Now the Crowthers gathered upstairs at the FDNY headquarters in Brooklyn, in a plain room with beige walls, alongside department officials, including Fire Commissioner Nicholas Scoppetta and Chief of Department Salvatore Cassano, the leaders of the FDNY.

"This is the least we could do," said Scoppetta. "He had everything to live for, and his parents can take comfort in the fact—if it's possible to take comfort under these circumstances—that he died while helping others."

Standing on the right side of the podium, facing the local news cameras and a small group of reporters, Jeff tried to stay composed. "We are honoring a true hero," Cassano said. "He had the genes of a New York City firefighter."

The commissioner and chief of the department named Welles a member, forever a part of its rolls, a brother among the bravest. At the end of the ceremony, Alison and Jeff were presented with a framed special commendation, a certificate of appointment for Welles, acknowledging his place in the ranks along with the more than eleven thousand others under the department's command. Proof that their son was recognized in a way he'd dreamed about since he was a boy.

Late one evening in May 2011, Alison was watching TV when President Obama stepped to a lectern in the White House to tell the nation and the world that Osama bin Laden was dead. After announcing the operation that killed the Al Qaeda leader, he harkened back to the terrorist attacks of September 11, 2001, remembering the Twin Towers of the World Trade Center falling; the crash of American Airlines Flight 77 into the Pentagon near Washington, D.C.; and the wreckage of United Flight 93 in Shanksville, Pennsylvania. Less than a minute into his remarks, his message grew more personal, his tone softer. He looked into the network pool camera, and spoke as if directly to the two people standing in a house in Upper Nyack.

"The worst images are those that were unseen to the world," the president said. "The empty seat at the dinner table. Children who were forced to grow up without their mother or their father. Parents who would never know the feeling of their child's embrace." They both listened, maybe even nodding, burdened with an understanding of such terrible truth.

At some point, the date occurred to them. May 1, 2011. It was Jeff and Alison's fortieth wedding anniversary.

The next morning, Alison was at the computer checking e-mail, still processing the president's remarks, when she received a message with an official-looking insignia attached. The note indicated that the president was preparing to visit ground zero, and stated that if she would like to attend a private event to meet him, she needed to provide pertinent information for a necessary background check. The message asked for her Social Security number and other personal material.

Scam, she thought. No way would she provide the information to a confusing, unknown sender with a government address, buried in an avalanche of letters and slashes. Her finger hovered over the delete key but then retreated. Her head was still buzzing with the president's speech and the notion of bin Laden gone. She clicked open the form and provided the information. She hit send and closed the screen.

Three days later, on a sunny windswept Thursday, Alison and Jeff traveled to Lower Manhattan. This was President Obama's first visit to the site since taking office. On previous anniversaries of the attacks, in 2009 and 2010, he'd paid his respects at the memorial at the Pentagon. This day, he came instead to the site where the overwhelming majority of lives were lost and to its deepest scar, to pay tribute to the victims of the attacks and to meet with their families as well as with firefighters, police officers, and other first responders. It was not a day for speeches. His presence was meant both as symbol and as salve—to honor those lost, and to represent justice done.

At the site where the Twin Towers once stood the president laid a wreath at the base of a tree recovered from amid the ruins, replanted, and somehow restored to full leaf. Afterward, he retreated to an area out of public view, without press. He visited the preview site for the 9/11 Memorial and Museum, set up across the street from St. Paul's Chapel on lower Broadway, the church that miraculously survived the terrorist attacks a block away without a single window broken. The chapel had served as refuge for those working at the site for months afterward, and stood to many as an emblem of God's grace.

In the preview center's simple setting, Jeff, Alison, and roughly sixty other family members of victims waited at tables of eight set up for the president's visit. All guests were checked and vetted, having passed facial recognition tests. Several early exhibits had already been designed and set up, awaiting transfer to the museum's permanent home, its opening still a few years away. One of the exhibits was dedicated to Welles. Jeff and Alison drifted to it as if to stand near him.

Just then, the door swung open and the president entered.

Alison was immediately struck by Barack Obama's presence, less formal, more radiant, different from the hundreds of times she'd seen him as an image on television, or pressed into a newspaper photo. She and Jeff had both been briefed about the visit. The president wanted to spend time with the families privately. Beyond that, they didn't know how much time he would spend, if they would speak to him directly. Here he was, on the other side of the room, so close, moving so easily from family to family, person to person, speaking with each one.

In the next moment, the president approached them, extending his hand, looking directly into their faces. Alison was clutching a red bandanna, squeezing it tightly in her hand, a piece not just of her son's life but of hers. Jeff put out his hand and said, "Mr. President, I'm the father of Welles Remy—" The president cut him off: "Crowther," he said.

"I know about your son," the president continued. "The man with the red bandanna."

"Thank you," Alison said, the first words that rushed out of her, looking at him. It wasn't gratitude for the acknowledgment. This came from a more primal, visceral place. "Thank you for getting the job done." She didn't feel she was speaking to a nation's leader right then, to the commander in chief who had ordered the mission.

"It was a feeling of one parent talking with another," she remembered years later. "Commiserating." As much as his praise for Welles's courage that day touched them, the president also spoke to them about their loss, and their coping. He told them he couldn't imagine losing one of his children, and marveled at the strength they possessed in enduring it.

As the president was about to leave, Alison didn't hesitate. She had to ask him a favor.

"Would you be willing to take a photo with us, Mr. President, near Welles's exhibit?" she asked. He agreed, telling them to stand by the display and wait for him there after he'd met with all the families in the room. They moved to the part of the room where Welles was memorialized and stood near his picture, wondering if Barack Obama would come back. He did.

He put his arms around Jeff and Alison and posed for a picture. And before leaving, Alison asked for one moment more. Would he be willing to sign a red bandanna for her? She had two ready.

The president reached for his pen, bent over, and signed the red fabric. Above his name, he inscribed a simple message.

"We won't forget Welles."

Drew Gallagher had first met Welles when they were college freshmen. Over the next four years, they crossed paths often. After graduating, when Welles went to Wall Street, Drew entered a field many of his buddies dreamed about but few ultimately pursued: sports. He landed a job at NESN, the New England Sports Network, one of the most successful regional sports broadcasters in the country. He worked there as a special projects coordinator for just three months before getting the call he most wanted. In February 2000, he joined ESPN as a production assistant.

The last time he'd seen Welles was on an escalator in Grand Central Terminal in the summer of 2001. They were moving in opposite directions, Drew headed up from the subway platforms and Welles headed down. They shouted their greetings to each other, the conversation swept away by the moving stairs. The encounter lasted less than fifteen seconds.

Drew first pitched the story about Welles to his bosses for the five-year anniversary of 9/11: the former athlete who died in the attacks after saving the lives of others caught in the South Tower. The bosses turned it down. Drew pitched ideas all the time, and only a handful were green-lit. He understood, but he didn't accept.

Over the next several years, he continued to pitch Welles's story. As a Boston College alum, he'd seen the Red Bandanna Run on campus grow steadily, and believed a longer feature on Welles's life would move people who'd never met him, simply through the valor and sacrifice of what he'd done. With the approach of the tenth anniversary, he pitched the story again. This time, the bosses gave the go-ahead.

Drew had already done a lot of preproduction work. I served as the reporter and writer for the feature, which was narrated by native New Yorker, actor, and director Ed Burns. The piece ran thirteen and a half minutes, debuting the first week of September 2011. The reaction came quickly.

"His story had come out," Alison said. "In the initial year there was media coverage, and every September 11 there was some talk of it. But once the ESPN story hit . . . wow. It launched . . ."

"Welles's story was out there," Paige said, "but the piece was the tipping point."

In the days following, the reaction grew and spread, nearly overwhelming the family. Teachers showed the piece to their students, coaches to their teams, parents to their children, and children to their parents, many of them writing letters to Jeff and Alison. A team in New Zealand competing in the Rugby World Cup wore red bandannas as a way to honor Welles. A news crew from France interviewed Jeff and Alison about the meaning of the symbol.

In the years to come, the piece would air every year on September 11. Posted on the Internet by dozens of sites, the video drew millions of views. Maybe some already knew the story, while others heard Welles's name for the first time. Maybe some were sports fans, while others were simply proud of one man's courage in the final measure of his life.

TEN

SHE'D NEVER RETURNED.

For more than thirteen years, she never came back. Even when she looked at his picture, frozen and ageless against time, sitting on a table next to the sofa in her living room in New Jersey, she didn't allow her mind to travel back. She focused only on the face and the name. Not the day. Not the place. Ling Young knew how difficult it would be to step back inside, to walk into the hollow where the towers once stood, across the ground where she once worked and so many friends and colleagues had perished. She came on this day not by her choice, but because of a friend's request.

Alison had asked her to come.

May 14, 2014, marked the long-awaited opening of the National September 11 Memorial and Museum in New York City. Its public unveiling would come in a week. This day was for a carefully selected crowd, seven hundred invited guests gathering far below ground, inside the museum's soaring central hall. The ceremony was set for broadcast around the country.

Alison would be called onstage, the first speaker to follow the president. He'd be introducing her, and Ling Young as well, the two women scheduled to walk to the stage together once the president finished his remarks.

The families arrived together, along with Honor, her husband, Rick, and their four children, and Paige and her fiancé, Jarrod. Their seats were in the second row, and walking to them they saw the names reserved for the chairs directly in front of theirs. Their seats were behind Bill and Hillary Clinton.

Jeff and Alison were in the same row, but across an aisle. Before the ceremony began, Alison and Ling were led from their seats to a place backstage behind a large screen set up for images to be displayed during the event. There was a monitor placed there, for them to watch what unfolded on the other side of the screen.

But it was the sound at the ceremony's start that reached inside Alison. A children's choir onstage and in an upper balcony began the program with a rendition of "Somewhere," from *West Side Story*, the play's most yearning anthem.

"When I heard the children sing," she said, "I started coming apart." She listened, trying to breathe deeply, to clear her mind, to focus on the short speech she'd written with Jeff, playing it through her memory. She was also deeply aware of Ling's nerves and apprehension, not only at being back here but at playing a role, coping with the weight of attention placed on her. Speaking in her second language, Ling was going to introduce Alison, her face and voice projected on the screen. They sat together, waiting to be called. They listened as an honor guard made its march down the center aisle, toward the stage, turning to face the assembly as the choir then sang the national anthem.

Michael Bloomberg, the former mayor of New York City, was the first to speak, and after brief remarks, he introduced Barack Obama to the stage.

Obama took long strides up the steps and moved behind the presidential lectern. He addressed the mayor, the governor, the guests, and the families of the fallen. Immediately after, he began to describe the scene on the 78th floor of the South Tower, mentioning the fire, the smoke, the darkness, the despair in the sky lobby's sudden wreckage. He paused, allowing the image to linger in the room.

"And then there came a voice," the president said. "Clear, calm, saying he had found the stairs. A young man in his twenties, strong, emerged from the smoke, and over his nose and his mouth he wore a red handkerchief."

Alison, behind the screen, felt the breath inside her seize. The president continued.

"He called for fire extinguishers to fight back the flames. He tended to the wounded. He led those survivors down the stairs to safety, and carried a woman on his shoulders down seventeen flights. Then he went back. Back up all those flights . . . bringing more wounded to safety. Until that moment when the tower fell. They didn't know his name. They didn't know where he came from. But they knew their lives had been saved by the man in the red bandanna."

The president spoke of the loss of nearly three thousand souls, saying the museum would forever provide a place "to touch their names and hear their voices and glimpse the small items that speak to the beauty of their lives."

But he singled out one life, and uttered one name, and described one man to the room, to the world.

"Welles was just twenty-four years old, with a broad smile and a bright future," the president said, as images of Welles flashed across the large screen behind him, the colors spilling into the space where Alison and Ling sat, waiting.

"He had a big laugh, a joy of life, and dreams of seeing the world. He worked in finance, but he had also been a volunteer firefighter. And after the planes hit, he put on that bandanna and spent his final moments saving others."

The speech lasted nine minutes, and at its conclusion, Obama called for the two guests waiting backstage to come forward.

"It is my honor to introduce two women forever bound by that day," the president said, "united in their determination to keep alive the true spirit of 9/11—Welles Crowther's mother, Alison, and one of those he saved, Ling Young."

As they emerged into view, holding hands as they climbed the tall steps toward the podium, the president turned toward them and began to clap, along with the rest of the audience. He greeted them, kissing Ling on the cheek, and then bending forward with a full reach to embrace Alison, her arms wrapping around him. Walking toward their separate lectern, Alison tried to remain composed, to keep her mind clear, with one goal, when she spoke.

"I wanted to show strength, not weakness," she said.

Ling began. "I'm here today because of Welles," she said, her voice strong and clear. "It was very hard for me to come here today, but I wanted to do so, so I could say thank you to his parents and my new friends, Jeff and Alison."

Alison looked at Ling, thanked her, and exhaled as she turned to the microphone. She spoke of her son in the present tense, not the past.

"My husband, Jefferson, and I could not be more proud of our son," she said. "For us, he lives on in the people he helped and in the memory of what he chose to do that Tuesday in September. Welles believes that we are all connected as one human family, that we are here to look out for and to care for one another."

From his seat in the second row, Jeff looked up at Alison and mouthed the words as his wife spoke them. Each had committed the speech to memory. As Alison continued, Jeff recited the lines silently, with tears in his eyes.

"It is our greatest hope," she said, her voice ringing through the hall, "that when people come here and see Welles's red bandanna, they will remember how people helped each other that day. And we hope that they will be inspired to do the same, in ways both big and small. This is the true legacy of September 11."

Welles's story has been documented on national television. His name has been said by a president. His number is worn on jerseys as a sign of honor, and his example has been made the foundation of a school curriculum. In so many ways, the memory of Welles Crowther lives on.

But none of that makes his absence any easier for his family. More than fifteen years later, his parents still mourn his death every day. "I weep for the loss of a potential that was unfulfilled. What he could have done in his lifetime had he lived long enough. I weep for the family he never had. But really," Jeff Crowther says, "I just weep for the loss of his company."

Welles with his father, Jefferson.

Welles didn't know it—nobody did—but in many ways, he had been preparing to save those lives in the South Tower his entire life. His instinct had always been to be a helper, whether he was cleaning the Empire Hook and Ladder Company No. 1 fire truck at eight years old, preventing a friend from getting in a fight in high school, or filling out his application to become a New York City firefighter as an adult working on Wall Street. On September 11, 2001, Welles made a choice that was second nature to him to help as many people as he could. And that choice is something everyone can learn from.

We all face choices every day. We choose how to treat our

parents, our siblings, our friends and peers. We choose when to speak up and when to be silent, when to fight and when to make peace. Often, these choices are small and might seem trivial. But they make us who we are.

Welles's final choice was to help. The next time you see a red bandanna, remember Welles—and imagine what the world would be like if we all chose to be helpers.

ACKNOWLEDGMENTS

IT IS NO SMALL request to ask a mother and father to share the territory of their lives, at once most precious and most painful, with a stranger. From the first moment I met Jefferson and Alison Crowther, they granted me an extraordinary trust. For this, I owe them far too much to repay or recount. Through dozens of interviews, phone calls, and visits to Upper Nyack, their memories became the living pulse of this narrative. Without them, this book would not be.

Thank you to Welles's sisters, Honor and Paige, for their time, honesty, and insight into Welles, and for traveling back into some of their brightest and hardest memories, to lend a shape to the past. And to the future, as Honor did in naming her first child Welles Remy Fagan, born in 2004.

As a portrait of strength and a proof of spirit, the Crowthers are as much a wonder as they are a family.

For information on the Welles Remy Crowther Trust, please visit www.crowthertrust.org. To learn about the educational and leadership curricula based on Welles's story, please visit www.redbandannaproject.org.

The idea for a fuller narrative of Welles's life came not from me, but from Scott Moyers at Penguin Press, who first saw its possibilities. He has worn every hat and played every role necessary in this book's creation. His endless patience, constant encouragement, and sure-handed editing have been as essential as air. Through the doubts, thanks for being mine in the struggle.

Also at Penguin Press, I am grateful for the contributions of the open-hearted Christopher Richards, for his careful and empathetic reading of the manuscript; Claire Vaccaro, for her strong and clear design; Darren Haggar, for creating so many versions of the evocative bandanna jacket; Sarah Hutson and Tessa Meischeid, house publicists who embraced this story before the pages were close to complete; Matt Boyd, the marketing maestro and an author's favorite voice of introduction; and Ann Godoff, who saw the good in this story and encouraged its place in the world.

David Black, literary agent and one of the toughest men I know, endured more than I can imagine in the time between receiving this book's proposal and its first manuscript, and always found time for support, counsel, and straight talk.

Thanks as well to Nick Khan at CAA, a consigliere more than an agent, whose interest and guidance from the book's commission to its completion were selfless and unflagging.

One of the first suggestions I received in the process was to enlist a good researcher. Here, I exceeded all advice by gaining the help of my colleague at ESPN William Weinbaum. To overstate Willie's contributions would be impossible, and to consider his work as research only would be entirely wrong. The best reporter I know, he served as the book's conscience and shepherd, its eyes and heart. The pages bear his imprint as much as mine.

I am grateful for those involved in the ESPN feature on Welles, without whose work this book would not have been written: Drew Gallagher, whose passion for the story came long before my own, and whose producing of the television piece remains a lesson to me in my work; Gregg Hoerdemann and his crew, who captured the indelible images that brought Welles's journey to life; Tim Horgan at Bluefoot, for his singular editing talent; and Victor Vitarelli, who oversaw the project and helped it reach its best form.

Also at ESPN, my gratitude goes to John Skipper and John Wildhack, for allowing me to pursue this story in a different venue.

Thanks, too, to all those who helped me at Sandler O'Neill, the firm that refused to fall. Over the past five years, Jimmy Dunne has been open and available at every turn. And to those employed there, then and still, who shared their memories of Welles and the stories of their survival, I am grateful.

To my brother, Robert, who worked for more than a decade on the eighty-first floor of the South Tower of the World Trade Center, and who left his office there in the spring of 2001, I am grateful. To my sister, Doretta, whose meeting across the street from the towers on September 11 was canceled early that morning, I am grateful for you too.

I wrote the majority of this book in the house my father, Ralph, built. I did most of the written work at his old desk. I'd like to believe his spirit has read these pages. I am beholden to him, forever.

My mother, Eileen, was my first and most faithful reader of the words written in that house nearly every day. Her encouragement and empathy, her patience and cheer were boundless and made a greater difference than I can ever describe. Thank you, Mom.

To our son, Jack, and our daughter, Tessa, you are the joyous purpose of all. To Dianne, to whom this book is dedicated: The door opens . . .

How will I do this?

You are how. And will be, always.

A NOTE ON SOURCES

FROM THE ORIGINAL telling of Welles's story as a television feature in 2011 through the completion of this narrative five years later, I am deeply indebted to many—for their time and memory, their work and care, their knowledge and patience, for their help in the reporting of this book.

I am grateful to the following for the interviews they granted and, in them, the insights and information they shared: Steve Addazio, Jessica Alberti, Marcie Baeza-Sauer, Michael Barch, Lee Burns, Matt Casamassima, Peter Cassano, Salvatore Cassano, Paige Crowther Charbonneau, Alison Crowther, Jefferson Crowther, Timothy Curry, James Devery, Matt Dickey, Matt Drowne, Scott Dunn, Jimmy Dunne, Tim Epstein, Honor Crowther Fagan, Chris Ferrarone, John Finlay, Karen Fishman, Mark Fitzgibbon, Drew Gallagher, James Gilroy, David Gottlieb, Jessica Quintana Hess, Jon Hess Willie Hopkins, Johnny Howells, Lee Ielpi, Tyler Jewell, Mary Jos, Stephen Joseph, Matt Katchmar, John Kline, Jane Lerner, George Leuchs, Rob Lewis, Susie DeFrancis Lind, Angelo

Mangia, Ben Marra, Pat McCavanagh, Natalie McIver, Dave Moreno, Ed Moy, Charles Murphy, Edward Nicholls, Keith O'Brien, Matthew O'Keefe, Justin Patnode, Nyack historian Win Perry, Chuck Platz, Karim Raoul, Chris Reynolds, Matt Rosen, John Ryan, John Scott, Jonathan Sperman, Jody Steinglass, Tom Sullivan, Gerry Sussman, Kevin Tiernan, James Tremble, Chris Varmon, Paul Wanamaker, Scott Wiener, and Ling Young.

Most of the interviews were transcribed and archived by NoNotes.com.

While the vast majority of this book comes from primary source material gained through interviews with those listed above, the reader surely understands the depth of reporting done on the September 11 attacks, across myriad outlets by hundreds, if not thousands, of journalists. Of those works, I leaned most heavily on several.

As mentioned in the text, *102 Minutes*, by Jim Dwyer and Kevin Flynn, was invaluable, not only in helping to convey the context around Welles's experience that day, but also in ways broader and more fundamental. The history of the towers, the intricacies of their design, the accounts of the survivors, and the painstaking chronology of those minutes between the first plane's strike and the second tower's fall are essential to any understanding of the day's events, and of Welles's movements that morning.

Also noted in the text, "Fighting to Live as the Towers Died," the Times's piece reported by Dwyer, Flynn, Eric Lipton, James Glanz, and Ford Fessenden, was the first mention of Welles, without name, as the man with the red handkerchief helping others on the 78th floor. In addition, the Times's accompanying piece, "Accounts from the South Tower," included vital interviews that aided in telling this story. In particular, Lipton's interview with Judy Wein and Fessenden's interview with Ling Young were essential in adding to the primary interviews done for this project.

A book that was especially important in helping to understand the challenges and dimension of the fallen towers, and the pile's unique horror, was William Langewiesche's singular *American Ground: Unbuilding the World Trade Center*. His chronicle of the recovery effort and the pile's clearing deeply informed this account.

For the plainest facts rooted in the attacks, most involving exact timings and numerical totals, I relied on *The Complete 9/11 Commission Report* (The National Commission on Terrorist Attacks upon the United States) as a definitive source.

The Press Office of the Fire Department of New York provided information, as did the New York City Fire Museum, about the FDNY and its posthumous honoring of Welles as a firefighter. And the Social Security Administration is the source for the data on newborns named Welles.

Terry Szuplat, the White House speechwriter who worked with President Obama on his remarks for the dedication of the 9/11 Memorial and Museum, given May 15, 2014, responded to our questions about the context and contents of the speech.

The Boston College athletic department was generous in its help and was an invaluable resource.

Welles's story was chronicled, in dozens of ways, long before I first learned of his valor. As mentioned in the text, Jane Lerner was the first to report his identity, as the man in the red bandanna, in her work for *The Journal News*, and played a key role in the nation's discovery of his actions.

I also owe a debt to the following journalists and their respective works, for the reporting that helped to provide greater context and important information on other subjects that played a role in Welles's story. In each case, the pieces were deeply helpful in the insights provided, during the research and writing of this book:

America Remembers, CNN special reports, 2002.

Bader, Jenny Lyn. "If You're Thinking of Living in: Nyack." *The New York Times*, August 14, 1988.

Batson, Bill. "Nyack Sketch Log: 150 Years of Volunteer Firefighting." *Nyack News & Views*, August 27, 2013.

Bianchi, Mike. "Red Bandanna Honoring 9-11 Hero Goes Perfectly with UCF School Colors." *Orlando Sentinel*, September 6, 2011.

Booker, Katrina. "After September 11: Starting Over." *Fortune*, January 21, 2002, updated September 11, 2015.

Cacioppo, Nancy. "Requiems for Victims: A Time for Prayer and Reflection." *The Journal News*, September 30, 2001.

Cauchon, Dennis. "For Many on 9/11, Survival Was No Accident." *USA Today*, December 20, 2001.

Dunlap, David. "A Close Bond and the Unending Toll of 9/11." *The New York Times*, June 8, 2012.

"The Heart of a Firefighter: 9/11 Hero Welles Crowther Named Honorary Firefighter," *FDNY News*, December 12, 2006.

Kolker, Robert. "The Long Good-Bye," *New York* magazine.

Lander, Mark. "Obama Honors Victims of Bin Laden at Ground Zero." *The New York Times*, May 5, 2011.

Lerner, Jane. "Volunteer Firefighter Found at Ground Zero Laid to Rest." *The Journal News*, March 31, 2002.

Littman, Adam. "Upper Nyack Dedicates Plaque to Harry Wanamaker Jr." *Nyack–Piermont Patch*, June 10, 2012.

Marine1fdny.com, website of Marine 1.

McFadden, Robert D. "Bosley Crowther, 27 Years a Critic of Films for Times, Is Dead at 75." *The New York Times*, March 8, 1981.

———. "Toni Morrison's Manuscripts Spared in Christmas Fire." *The New York Times*, December 28, 1993.

Morales, Tatiana. 2002. "Her Heroes," CBS News, September 4, 1993.

New York Times staff. *Portraits: 9/11/01—The Collected "Portraits of Grief" from* The New York Times. New York: Times Books, 2002.

Nocera, Joe. "After 5 Years, His Voice Can Still Crack." *The New York Times*, September 9, 2006.

Perry, Alison. "Postcard from NY: Iconic Images." *Nyack News & Views*, June 24, 2012.

Robbins, Liz. "Hudson River Rescue Still Defines Upgrade of Fire Dept.'s Marine Unit." *The New York Times*, January 14, 2011.

Rosaforte, Tim, and Bill Fields. "A Year of Living Gratefully." *Golf Digest*, December 2002.

Thamel, Pete. "Boston College Uses Emotion and Its Running Game to Shock No. 9 USC." SI.com, September 14, 2014.

Wells, Julia. "A Man of the Land, Ozzie Fischer Jr. Dies on Island He Nurtured for Nine Decades." *Vineyard Gazette*, July 28, 2011.

Whitford, David. "Sandler O'Neill's Journey from Ground Zero." *Fortune*, September 1, 2011.

Zawacki, Kevin. "Fatally Stabbed Nyack Man Remembered as Teammate, Served Time for Assault." Patch.com, June 27, 2011.

DISCUSSION QUESTIONS

1. Welles always had a clear and confident answer whenever someone asked him about his future. He knew what he wanted to do. What goals do you have for the future? What are some steps you can take to make them happen?

2. What are some of the qualities that make someone a hero? In your opinion, was Welles Crowther a hero? If yes, why?

3. Welles carried his red bandanna with him everywhere. Do you have something (a piece of jewelry, a book, etc.) in your life that is important to you?

4. After 9/11, a memorial was built to honor the victims at the World Trade Center site. Why do you think it is important to have public memorials?

5. Welles Crowther once said, "I'm a superhero" (pg. 49). What qualities do you have that would make you a good hero in your everyday, normal life?

6. Have you ever lost someone important to you? How do you keep their memory alive?

7. Imagine for a moment that you are face-to-face with your biggest fear. What actions can you take to be brave and overcome your fear?

8. When the Twin Towers were attacked, many people survived because they were able to follow protocol to find the quickest way to safety. Do you know what to do at school and at home in case of an emergency? Please take a moment to refresh safety instructions or make a plan with a teacher and your parent/guardian.

9. Both of Welles's grandfathers would take him to the fire station as a child. It was a tradition. Do you have any family traditions? Please describe.

10. Welles was taught, "You must help those in danger" (pg. 6). As a kid, it is not your responsibility to help someone in danger, but in some instances, you can still take action. What are some ways you can help someone in danger without interfering directly and while keeping yourself safe?

11. Welles once gave in to peer pressure and did something dangerous (pg. 14) even though he knew it was wrong. Have you ever given in to peer pressure? What are some ways you can stand up to peer pressure?

12. Welles became known as the Man in the Red Bandanna. It was a part of him. Is there something that is not part of your physical appearance, but is very much part of who you are?

13. In your own words, what is Welles Crowther's legacy? What do you want your legacy to be?